"*The Long Game* offers a thoughtful, practical, and compelling approach to achieving one's higher ambitions in a demanding, short-term-focused world. A very worthy read."

—**DOUG CONANT,** founder and CEO, ConantLeadership; Chairman, CECP; former CEO, Campbell Soup Company

"If you want to take control of your life and career—and cultivate the habits for success—read *The Long Game*."

—**CHARLES DUHIGG,** bestselling author, *The Power of Habit* and *Smarter Faster Better*

"To redefine success on your own terms and build a life that matters, read *The Long Game*."

—**KEITH FERRAZZI,** *New York Times* bestselling author, *Never Eat Alone* and *Leading Without Authority*

"This is one of those rare books that can help us refocus on what truly matters. Masterfully written and packed with actionable advice, Dorie Clark's *The Long Game* shows us how to break the every-day-is-a-sprint cycle and discover our comfortable, personal marathon pace."

—**FRANCESCA GINO,** Tandon Family Professor of Business Administration, Harvard Business School; bestselling author, *Rebel Talent*

"If you're interested in building and living a truly meaningful life, this wonderful précis by my extraordinary friend Dorie Clark is for you. It's full of specific, actionable advice that you'll be able to apply immediately."

—**HUBERT JOLY,** former Chairman and CEO, Best Buy; Senior Lecturer of Business Administration, Harvard Business School; and author, *The Heart of Business*

"Be prepared never to look at your life the same way again. *The Long Game* is a must-read for anyone desperate to be liberated from the shackles of the screen and discover a life post-Covid."

—**MARTIN LINDSTROM,** bestselling author,
The Ministry of Common Sense and Buy·ology

"Success is not a question of how much stuff you get done. It's not even a question of what you manage to achieve. Instead, it's knowing your purpose in life and taking the right steps to fulfill your potential. Dorie Clark is one of my favorite writers, and *The Long Game* may be her best book yet. Filled with inspiring examples and practical advice for how to approach your career differently, this book will quite literally change your life. I highly recommend it."

—**ERIN MEYER,** author, *The Culture Map*; coauthor,
No Rules Rules; and Professor of Management Practice, INSEAD.

The Long Game

The Long Game

How to be a long-term thinker in a short-term world

BY DORIE CLARK

HARVARD BUSINESS REVIEW PRESS
BOSTON, MASSACHUSETTS

The web addresses referenced in this book were live and correct at the time of the book's publication but may be subject to change.

Library of Congress Cataloging-in-Publication Data

Names: Clark, Dorie, author.
Title: The long game : how to be a long-term thinker in a short-term world / by Dorie Clark.
Description: Boston, MA : Harvard Business Review Press, [2021] |
    Includes index.
Identifiers: LCCN 2021009351 (print) | LCCN 2021009352 (ebook) |
ISBN 9781647820572 (hardcover) | ISBN 9781647820589 (ebook)
Subjects: LCSH: Planning. | Career development. | Quality of life.
Classification: LCC HD30.28 .C555 2021 (print) | LCC HD30.28
    (ebook) | DDC 658.4/09—dc23
LC record available at https://lccn.loc.gov/2021009351
LC ebook record available at https://lccn.loc.gov/2021009352

ISBN: 978-1-64782-057-2
eISBN: 978-1-64782-058-9

The paper used in this publication meets the requirements of the American National Standard for Permanence of Paper for Publications and Documents in Libraries and Archives Z39.48-1992.

*To my mother, Gail Clark, and to the
Recognized Expert community.
You inspire me every day.*

Contents

SECTION THREE

Keeping the Faith

The Long Game

Introduction

I bolted out of bed at the sound—sharp, insistent. It was still dark, and I was disoriented. What was happening in the middle of the night?

And then I remembered.

It was 3:30 a.m., and the piercing sound was my alarm. I'd set it the night before, because I had a 5 a.m. flight to catch at JFK.

Downing two aspirin—I already had a headache—I tossed on the clothes I'd laid out on the dresser and summoned my Uber. Heading over the deserted Brooklyn Bridge, I stared at the hundreds of office building lights—left blazing all night—that twinkled against the lapping East River below. I had a mission to accomplish. All I needed to do was force my body to comply.

I could rest a little on the plane, then prep for my day of meetings in Los Angeles. I'd arrive at the client by 9:30 a.m. Pacific and sit in on meetings until 6 p.m. (9 p.m. back home), followed by a quick dinner before bed. The next day I'd have more meetings in

LA, capped by a flight to Atlanta, arriving at 5:50 p.m. Eastern. If weather and traffic held, I'd have just enough time to reach my client dinner meeting and then give a keynote talk the next morning.

I knew I could do it all—I had to. And that week, it all went off without a hitch. But speeding across the Brooklyn Bridge, I felt a quick, sharp stab. For just a moment, before I could tamp it down, it felt like loneliness. For just a moment, I wondered why I decided my life should be this way.

O X O O

Around that time, I was teaching a business school executive education program. A large financial services firm had brought in thirty of its top performers for a special two-day session. These men and women were some of the most successful people at the company, but when I chatted with them after the workshop, they had a common refrain: "I just wish I had time to think."

It was something I'd been hearing a lot lately, even from the people closest to me. My best friend owed me a response to a document I'd sent over. She was usually prompt and thorough—but lately, not so much.

"It's a quick read when you get a chance to take a breath," I texted her, by way of encouragement.

"Taking a breath is the issue," she wrote back from her out-of-state business trip.

By all outside measures, she was doing great, with a thriving business and a new relationship. But inside, she felt she was barely keeping up.

O✗O O

So many of us today feel rushed, overwhelmed, and perennially behind. We keep our heads down, always focused on the next thing. We're stuck in permanent "execution mode," without a moment to take stock or ask questions about what we really want from life.

Flicking through our friends' and colleagues' social media feeds in spare moments, we're taunted by a parade of triumphs: *What's their secret? What do they know that I don't? Why aren't I keeping up? Isn't there a "life hack" out there that can help?*

It's no way for any of us to live.

What would it look like to set aside comparison, discover our own definition of success, and live life on our own terms? The patience, strategy, and consistent effort required to get there may seem like lost art forms. But to create the kind of interesting, meaningful lives that we all seek, they're essential—and it's time to embrace them.

O✗O O

On February 28, 2020, my email pinged. "I'm delighted to report that we would love to publish the book," my editor wrote. *The Long Game* was on.

The very next day—March 1, 2020—the first case of Covid-19 was diagnosed in New York City, where I live.

During the early days of lockdown, a colleague messaged me about my book project. I had set out to write about the importance of being a long-term thinker in a short-term world. But in light of

Covid, he wondered, wasn't long-term thinking a little passé? The real issue, he said, was "what's likely to change unexpectedly and bite any long-term thinking in the ass."

I'd been focused on combating the destructive lure of short-term thinking. But now, in the midst of a pandemic where everything changed overnight, the question flipped: *Was long-term thinking even relevant anymore?*

O X O O

As New York City hospitals overflowed during those early months, the health risks of Covid were terrifying. So were the financial implications. My spring travel plans had been set for months: teaching in Moscow, plus keynote talks in Dallas, Vancouver, Florida, and more. Those trips—and the income they would have generated—were completely vaporized.

But then I realized: I knew what to do. My speaking business began in 2013, with the launch of my first book, *Reinventing You*. Keynote speaking is lucrative, and can be glamorous: talks have brought me around the globe.

And yet, I knew it wasn't always going to be sustainable. I knew it when I embarked on a three-city speaking tour of Slovakia, muscling through despite a hacking cough and laryngitis. I knew it when I taught six hours a day for two weeks at a business school in Kazakhstan, despite a high fever and chills. When a client has brought you so far, the show must go on, and I always delivered. But I also knew that one day, if I ever got *really* sick, it might not happen. I had friends, only in their thirties, diagnosed with immune system disorders or cancer. *God forbid*, I thought. But it made me want to plan.

The secret, I knew, was to find a way to earn money that didn't depend on my physical presence—to stop "trading time for dollars." So in 2014, I started experimenting with online courses. Working with an established company, I created my first course that year, and I partnered with a different company in 2015 to create a second. I was experimenting, learning.

Finally, in 2016, I decided to go all in: I'd independently create my own online course, and to ensure I did it the right way, I'd write a book about the process of carving out new revenue streams, interviewing the world's experts along the way. It was an immersive research project and became my book *Entrepreneurial You*, released in 2017.

I certainly didn't see a pandemic coming—that's not why I started investigating how to develop side gigs and multiple sources of revenue. I was a lot more concerned about the prosaic: falling ill, or perhaps just getting tired of life on the road. The truth is, none of us can predict the future. But we can certainly identify goals we want to head toward, or potential vulnerabilities we want to avoid.

In the two months after Covid hit, I turned up the volume on projects and relationships I'd been developing over the prior six years. I wrote the scripts for, and filmed, three new online courses and led a large-scale relaunch of my own online course, Recognized Expert. Those efforts, thankfully, enabled me to turn what could have been a disastrous year for my business into its most successful to date.

Doubling down on online courses may have been a short-term move. But it wasn't born of short-term thinking. None of what I accomplished would have been possible without the strategic pivot toward digital education I'd been executing for more than half a decade. Long-term thinking protects us during downturns (of all kinds), because it keeps us moving toward our most important goals.

We need to be nimble, and adapt when circumstances change. But long-term thinking is what undergirds everything and enables us to make those adjustments. If all we do is bumble along, reacting to stimuli, we won't be anywhere near our goals. But if, instead, we embrace long-term strategy and recognize that the path may change over time—that's what maximizes our chances of success.

Long-term thinking isn't dead, I realized. Not by a long shot.

OXOO

Taking the long view also has an unusual side effect: courage. My friend Martin Lindstrom is a top branding consultant and advises one of the world's royal families. The monarch pulled him aside during one visit: "Mr. Lindstrom," he said, "don't be short-sighted. I want you to think in the long term."[1]

How long?

"We're not interested in the next couple of months," the ruler told Martin. "We don't make quarterly earnings announcements. We don't even operate with a midterm horizon of five or ten years. We operate with a lifelong horizon, one generation at a time. In your strategic branding work for my family, if one generation does well, you've accomplished your job."

That perspective is vanishingly rare these days. For example, plenty of companies have been caught flat-footed in recent years around social issues from race relations to marriage equality to climate change. But it usually isn't because their leaders disagree with the premise. As Martin notes, "Through my career, I've come to know hundreds of CEOs, and not one of them—I mean, zero—has ever disagreed with the concept of equality." What's driving their awkward responses is often fear of the short-term consequences, whether it's a hit to quarterly earnings, a dip in stock price, or a slashed year-end bonus.

It takes courage to be a long-term thinker, and a willingness to buck the near-term consequences. But the payoff can be enormous.

My friend Jonathan Brill is an innovation expert in Silicon Valley. The real risk for companies, he told me, "is that you hire smart people who know how to win—and you tell them to win at the wrong thing." When all the incentives point toward short-term revenue goals, that's what executives optimize for. "The result of that," Jonathan says, "is that you can lose by winning."

You lose because instead of investing in meaningful innovation that can transform your company or your industry, you invest in what's known as "feature innovation"—as in, "What color button should I put on that new box?" A new color on a box doesn't revolutionize anything, and it won't last. But it's easy, and it might marginally improve outcomes right now.

Everyone loves 10x returns and the luster of breakthrough innovation, of course. But the problem is, it takes time. "It takes typically five or six years for a product or a business to get to scale," Jonathan says. There's a ramp-up period to see if things are working, to adjust, and to optimize. For a long time, even some of the best innovations can look like sinkholes where money goes to die. But once they're established, you've built a powerful competitive moat. Ultimately, he says, "What you're looking for is profit. That happens on the decade scale. That doesn't happen on the quarterly scale."

It's only long-term thinking that will get you there. And it turns out the same principle that works for the best and smartest corporations also works in our own lives.

OXOO

It was 2008, in the heady weeks before the financial crash. I'd managed to talk my way into an elite conference where I didn't know anyone and was probably the least qualified person in the room. I found a group of people about my age and—victory!— cadged an invitation to join them for dinner. They all knew one another, because they'd all gone to the same Ivy League college.

As we waited for the appetizers to arrive, one woman started a conversation about whether, a decade out of school, people in their class had produced more babies or books. For what seemed like several hours, they ticked through the names of people they all knew: This one had a baby. That one had written a book. This one was expecting. That one had written *five* books! And on and on.

Back then I had zero babies and zero books. All I could do was smile pleasantly and think: *f*@% you.*

There's a great quote by Henry Wadsworth Longfellow that goes something like: we measure ourselves by what we feel capable of doing, while others measure us based on what we've done. This makes sense, of course. But it's awfully frustrating when there's a gap between what we know we can accomplish and what we've done up to that point.

Everything takes longer than we want it to. Everything.

OXOO

By the start of the next year, I had a plan: land a book contract in the coming twelve months, no matter what. I was relentless and spent the spring writing three different book proposals. A publisher was going to want one of them, I was sure, but I wasn't going to take any chances. Through a friend, I managed to hook up with a literary agent. She rejected one proposal out of the gate—"It's an article, not a book," she told me—but thought the other two *might* have merit. Over the summer, I revised them endlessly, polishing my prose and sharpening my ideas until we had something distinct to send to publishers.

Except no one wanted them, either. Rejection after rejection came streaming in, with the same feedback: *good try, but you're not famous enough*. My agent eventually gave up and dropped me.

I decided to start blogging (which I didn't want to do), so I could eventually get "famous enough" to be able to write a book. It took an additional two years of pitching myself to publications, begging friends for introductions, and enduring a stream of editors who blew me off. But I finally built up enough articles, and momentum, to land a book deal. And two years after that, *Reinventing You* was finally released.

It had been a long time since that humiliating dinner conversation. But finally, I was able to share my ideas with the world.

O X O O

For every success, there are plenty of times when something we wanted or strove for didn't work out. But equally, along the way, there are times worth savoring. Moments when you realize the small steps that felt frustrating and arduous, and maybe even pointless at the time, were the ones that made the difference.

The challenge for all of us is an inner one: to keep going when it seems like no one is paying attention or cares. And to believe that eventually the world will catch up.

OXOO

A few years ago, I launched Recognized Expert,[2] an online course and community for talented professionals to learn how to build their platform so they can share their ideas with the world. Every day, I see participants face the same challenges I went through. There are times to celebrate, but also times when the pitch is rejected, the proposal is turned down, or the application to present never even gets a response. Meanwhile, the endless barrage on social media makes it clear: everyone else seems to have it figured out.

We can't help but wonder: *Should I be hustling faster? Grinding more? Crushing it harder? Why isn't it working?* For most of us, we're already hustling as hard and as fast as we possibly can. For many professionals, there's literally no margin. We're so caught up in execution mode, it feels like there's barely even time to think. So what can we do?

OXOO

There are two things I hate in this world. One of them is patience. My entire childhood, I resented being told I couldn't drive, or open a business, or vote. I didn't want to wait for my life to start mattering. But I've made my peace with patience, because everything meaningful I've done has required far more time than I wanted or anticipated. The five years between being in that "how many books" conversation and publishing my first one felt like a shameful eternity. Why was it taking so long?

And yet it came, eventually. I've come to understand what few recognize: the rate of payoff for persevering during those dark days isn't linear. It's exponential.

It took five years, on the surface, to show *any progress at all* between that dinner conversation and actually having a book to show for it. But in the half decade after that, I managed to build a seven-figure business, become a professor at two of America's top business schools, and have my books translated into eleven languages. I also became a Broadway investor, a stand-up comedian, and a producer of a Grammy-winning jazz album on the side.

If it were easy to be patient, and easy to do the work, then everyone would do it. What I've come to love about patience is that, ultimately, it's the truest test of merit: *Are you willing to do the work, despite no guaranteed outcome?* We earn our success by toiling without recognition, accolades, or even any certainty that it's going to come to fruition. We have to take it on faith and do it anyway. That's *strategic patience.* You have to surround yourself with people you admire and trust, and learn from their example. You have to study what's worked before and what you wish to emulate, and then determine where you want to do something different.

And you have to be willing—and so many aren't—to make choices. To recognize that saying "yes" to one thing inevitably means saying "no" to something else. You have to weigh those consequences and put your chips on the table. Trying to do it all means nothing of substance will ever get done.

But the power of consciously choosing how we're going to spend our time—and therefore our lives—is monumental. You have to place your bets, make your move, and wait. So I've become OK with patience.

O X O O

What I haven't become OK with—the second thing I hate—is information hoarding. So often, the people who have succeeded pull up the ladder behind them. For them, it's better to stick to the conventional heroic narrative: *brilliance and talent got recognized!* No need to dirty your hands with tactics, or scrap to succeed, when you're so exceptional.

Except no one is that exceptional.

I knew a very successful artist, the kind who spoke at TED and landed major international commissions. I asked her how she broke through: *What was her secret?*

Just do great work, she said.

If only. Great work is necessary, of course. But it's a starting point. You and I all know talented people—just as good as the pros—who never made it. There are always steps, techniques, strategies. But when those who have already made it don't share what they know? No one else really learns what it takes. The process remains shrouded in secrecy. That makes me angry.

We all know the mantra: there's no such thing as an overnight success. We know it takes time and patience. But what I've come to discover, in my executive coaching work and with participants in my Recognized Expert community, is that often it's unclear what "patience" means. Is patience writing two articles? Ten? A hundred? A thousand? How long until we get our ideas recognized and are able to create the kind of lives and careers we want?

In *The Long Game*, my goal is to lay the process bare and to share the unvarnished reality behind what it takes to build long-term success.

OXOO

The first step is understanding that the key to a meaningful life is to set our own terms for it. Financial success is certainly something that most of us strive for. But it should never be the only metric. Instead, we need to think broadly about how we want to grow and develop as people, and how to interlace those themes into our lives.

The other step is understanding that we can attain almost anything we want—but not instantly. If we're methodical, if we're persistent, and if we take small, deliberate steps, we can arrive there. The going may be slow at first, but the advantages of those actions, compounded over time, can lead to stunning results.

Playing the long game—eschewing short-term gratification in order to work toward an uncertain but worthy future goal—isn't easy. But it's the surest path to meaningful and lasting success in a world that so often prioritizes what's easy, quick, and ultimately shallow.

In this book, I'll be sharing key concepts and strategies that undergird the process of long-term thinking—ones that I've discovered through experimentation in my own life, as well as through coaching hundreds of top executives and entrepreneurs.

This book is intended for professionals who want something more out of their lives and work, and who are willing to take the harder path to get there. You may be a midcareer executive, like Jenny, wondering what's next. You could be an entrepreneur, like Ron, frustrated that your ideas aren't being heard as widely as you wish. You could be planning for a retirement career, like Albert, and don't want to waste time or energy with the wrong moves. You might be a younger professional, like Marie, ready to play on a bigger stage (metaphorical or literal—in chapter 3, you'll hear about Marie's journey to performing at the legendary Carnegie Hall).

The book is divided into three sections: "White Space," "Focus Where It Counts," and "Keeping the Faith."

In section one, White Space, we'll start with an often-overlooked part of playing the long game: the need to clear the decks first. If you're too busy and frenzied to think, then it's almost impossible to break out of a short-term mindset.

In chapter 1, we'll talk about the *real* reason we're all so busy. You have too much to do, it's true. But it's also true that our stuffed calendars tend to be a prison of our own making. We'll discuss practical tools you can use to escape—or at least jam open the bars a little wider. And in chapter 2, we'll turn to specific ways you can get more comfortable saying no, so that you can create more room in your calendar to do what's most important.

Section two, "Focus Where It Counts," gets to the heart of long-term thinking. How do we identify the right goals to go after, and how can we pursue them strategically and effectively, given the other serious demands on our time?

In chapter 3, we'll discuss frameworks you can use to identify the right goals for you—and I'll make the case for why you should "optimize for interesting." Chapter 4 centers around the concept, popularized by Google, of "20% time," meaning you spend one-fifth of your time on new ideas and projects. I'll share examples of professionals who applied this strategy in their own lives and why it's important for all of us to set aside time for experimentation. Chapter 5 addresses a common objection: *I want to do it all, but I don't know where to start!* We'll talk about how to map out your implementation strategy using a concept I call *thinking in waves.*

Chapter 6 is all about getting smarter with how we spend our time. Is there a way to kill two birds with one stone and leverage our time and energy more efficiently to achieve our goals? It turns out there is. The section concludes with chapter 7, which explains why building a strong network is critical to playing the long game and why so many people hesitate to do it. I'll lay out a framework that can help you think through how to build genuine relationships—and not feel sleazy during the networking process.

Finally, in section three, "Keeping the Faith," we'll turn to what is often the hardest part about playing the long game: moving forward despite challenges or setbacks.

In chapter 8, we'll discuss strategic patience, the key to persevering when you've hit a plateau (or even, at times, when it feels like you're slipping backward). Chapter 9 takes on failure, which usually feels awful and humiliating, Silicon Valley's "fail fast" ideology notwithstanding. The secret is understanding the crucial difference between failure and experimentation—because if you're learning, you're not actually failing.

Finally, in chapter 10, we'll talk about the final step: reaping the rewards of your hard work. Ironically, that's not always easy for successful people. Over the years, you grow accustomed to striving and hustling, and it can be hard to pull back and actually stop and savor the moment. But playing the long game today means building the kind of long-term career success that enables you to look back with satisfaction and joy at the life you've created.

OXOO

Intellectually, we all know that lasting success takes persistence and effort. And yet, so much of our culture pushes us toward doing what's easy, what's guaranteed, and what looks glamorous in the moment. *The Long Game* is intended to be a clarion call on behalf of long-term thinking. It's a practical tool kit that shows you—in those darkest moments of doubt—how to keep prioritizing what matters most, doing small things over time to achieve your goals, and being willing to keep at them, even when they seem pointless, boring, or hard.

Those are the choices that set you apart. It's blogging when no one reads your blog, to test ideas and create an audience. It's taking the Toastmasters class when it seems like no one cares what you have to say, to become a more effective presenter. It's going to networking events when you feel like the least accomplished person in the room, to gain new insights and contacts.

You can't perceive a difference after a week or a month or (often) even a year. Big goals may seem—and frankly *are*—impossible in the short term. But what few realize is that with small, methodical steps taken day after day, almost anything is attainable, and frequently sooner than you might imagine.

So let's start playing the long game.

Section One

White Space

OOXOOO

You can't pour more liquid into a glass that's already full. And that's why, if we're going to make smart choices about how to spend our time and energy, we need to give ourselves some white space.

Too many talented professionals live their lives on autopilot, racing around from one obligation to another. Being so busy may seem like the path to success—but without time to reflect, an ominous possibility looms: What if we're optimizing for the wrong things? We need to give ourselves the opportunity to explore what a successful life means to *us*. That's what we cover in the next two chapters.

1

The Real Reason We're All So Busy

We all know that rushing around and living eternally in the short term isn't optimal. In fact, in a study of senior leaders by the Management Research Group,[1] 97% identified strategic thinking—the ability to focus deliberately on long-term priorities—as key to their organization's success.

But something's getting in the way. In a separate study,[2] almost the exact same percentage of respondents—96%—claimed they don't have enough time to do long-term strategic thinking.

Really?

There's no question that professionals today are busy. A McKinsey study shows knowledge workers spend a full 28% of their time processing email,[3] and a separate study by the Atlassian Group says that professionals attend an average of sixty-two meetings per month[4]—which sounds like a shocking number, until you realize it breaks down to about two or three meetings per workday. That's not unusual; that's just Tuesday.

The frenzy of scurrying from appointment to appointment, writing report after report, taking an occasional selfie (hi, internet!), and then answering emails until midnight begins to feel like we're living our own personal *Groundhog Day*. Meanwhile, our real work—the work we get evaluated on, and that actually accomplishes something—is what gets sandwiched in between.

The truth is, some firms still erroneously conflate face time at the office (or "screen time" if you're working virtually) with productivity and company loyalty. Research shows that employees who log fifty or more hours per week earn 6% more compared with their less-zealous colleagues,[5] even though productivity actually *decreases* after fifty hours.[6] So the "always on" mentality is a rational adaptation to those misplaced incentives.

But that's not the whole story. When 96% of high-achieving leaders say they just can't get around to something mission-critical, something else is going on.

The Hidden Benefits of Frenzy

We say we want white space in our calendar and time to think. After all, we constantly feel on the brink of falling behind. We're always looking ahead to the next thing on the calendar and are never able to enjoy what's in front of us. Even the best job becomes miserable if the pace is too frenetic, the demands too overwhelming, and the pressure too unyielding.

So why can't we stop?

It turns out that we may be deriving hidden benefits from our relentless, short-term "execution mode." Research from Silvia

Bellezza of Columbia Business School and her colleagues showed that being busy, at least in the United States, signals high social status. "Individuals who possess the human capital characteristics that employers or clients value (e.g., competence and ambition) are expected to be in high demand and short supply on the job market. Thus, by telling others that we are busy and working all the time, we are implicitly suggesting that we are sought after, which enhances our perceived status."[7]

In other words, being "crazy busy"—and making sure others know it—may, consciously or subconsciously, be important to our self-esteem. And though we long for the time to do long-term thinking, possessing it may signal we're just a little less essential than we thought we were.

Self-worth is certainly a powerful incentive for us to keep busy. But it's not the only one.

Numbing Out

Busyness is also, it turns out, an anesthetic. The author Tim Ferriss, in an interview on his podcast, *The Tim Ferriss Show*, talked about how "up until at least 2004, my solution to feeling anything I didn't want to feel was to add more activities . . . to drown it out. Some people use heroin, some people use coke, some people use work. And I used activities."[8]

I've certainly done the same. Several years ago, reeling from a breakup and a death in my family, I sold my house, moved to another state, and still managed to deliver sixty-one keynote talks that year. More than once a week, I clambered into yet another taxi, boarded yet another plane, and traveled to yet another hotel ballroom. And I loved it, because being away from my home was the only time I wouldn't cry. I could focus on the mechanics: which airline, which terminal, which gate. I could focus on delivering my talk and pleasing the client. Even the logistics—where to find good Indian food in Cincinnati or Phoenix or Charlotte—helped distract me. Because when I got back home and found myself alone, it was often more than I could bear.

There's great existential comfort in feeling that *you know what to do.* When we're busy and focused on execution, there's no time to ask questions that might have discomfiting answers. *Is this the right path? What does success really mean? Am I living my life the way I want to?* If you need to grow revenue by 25% but don't know how, or need to reevaluate your career choices, or have to cope with industry disruption, it's much easier to keep doing the same thing and insist you just don't have time for a reappraisal of your business, or your life.

That was the case for Ali Davies, a self-employed consultant in Canada. Originally from England, Ali had a successful corporate career for fourteen years, but "at about the ten-year mark, I was feeling unsettled and unhappy," she told me. "I knew I wanted out, but kept convincing myself to stay. I was 'successful,' and [there was] fear of what that would mean for my identity if I turned my back on the conventional definition of success, and fear of it being the 'wrong' decision."

Ali ended up staying in her corporate career for another four years before she "did eventually start asking myself the questions that needed to be asked." She adds, "Sometimes the stories we tell ourselves about our professional lives hold us back if we don't dissect what's going on."

Rebecca Zucker knows the feeling well. Fresh out of Stanford's business school and working for Goldman Sachs, she already had a sterling résumé. "I was interviewing with [BNP] Paribas in Paris," she says. "I remember telling the head of M&A that all I wanted to do was M&A, when all I wanted to do was cry," she recalls. "He set me up with ten more interviews that I kept doing."

So often, we identify a path of what worked before, or what *should* work, or what we *should* want—and we stick to it at all costs, even when it makes us miserable. Eventually, Rebecca had a revelation: "I didn't give a shit about banking. I just wanted to be in Paris." Who we really are, or what we actually want to do, may seem obvious in retrospect. But as humans in a society that lionizes being busy, it's not always easy to tap into that understanding.

In 1971, Herbert Simon, a professor of computer science and psychology at Carnegie Mellon, made a prescient prediction. "In an information-rich world," he said, "the wealth of information creates a dearth of something else . . . the attention of its re-cipients."[9] The solution was clear: "to allocate that attention ef-ficiently among the overabundance of information sources that might consume it." In other words, we have to get smart about what we focus on.

Simon was speaking twenty-five years before the internet—in its rudimentary, dial-up form—entered most Americans' lives. And now, a quarter century after that, we're realizing just how hard focusing our attention really is. We live in a world where the lure of short-term thinking—just keeping our heads down and *doing*, again and again—is pervasive. Our workplaces push us to-ward it, and often, so does our own psychology.

Senior corporate leaders are almost unanimous that long-term strategic thinking is crucial. (When was the last time 97% of any-one agreed on anything?) So, if we *do* agree with that premise, where do we begin?

Changing Our Perspective

The reclamation may start with Derek Sivers.

Sivers began his career as a musician and morphed into an entrepreneur when he created an online independent music company called CD Baby, which he successfully sold in 2008. But unlike many entrepreneurs, who plow headfirst into another startup or angel investing, Sivers took a different path, moving abroad (Singapore; New Zealand; Oxford, England) and devoting most of his time to writing.

To him, being busy isn't a mark of status: it's a mark of servitude. "I have a very negative impression of the stereotypical frazzled, freaked-out, 'Oh my God, I'm so busy!' type," he told me. "They seem out of control—not in control of their life. But I've met a few super-successful people that are calm, collected, unbothered, and give you their full attention. They seem to have everything under control. So, I'd rather be like that."

Changing our perspective on whom we admire is a powerful first step. But, of course, even if we respect people who have total discretion over their schedule and plenty of time for what's most important, that doesn't mean it's easy to become them.

Even the least-connected professional probably has more requests than she can manage in a week (invitations for lunch, dinner, video calls, project meetings, catch-up sessions, "brain picking" requests, asks for advice and introductions, and more). Saying no to some is mandatory: you literally can't fit them all in. But to say no to all of them, or almost all of them, in order to create white space . . . that may feel close to impossible. What about hurting people's feelings? What about missing opportunities?

It's not easy, which is why the entirety of the next chapter is about how to say no—even to good things. But the key is this: if we venerate busyness, even subconsciously, we'll make decisions that lead us in that direction. Instead, we need to get clear on what we want. And if it's true mastery over our schedule, and the ability to plan and think that comes along with that, then we need to step up and be brave enough to choose accordingly.

That's what Dave Crenshaw did.

Planning around Your Priorities

"It wasn't a great environment that I grew up in," Dave told me. "So I wanted to provide something different for my kids." He knew that even back in college, more than twenty years ago. He remembers a class where his professor asked everyone to write out a vision for their future life. Dave's dream was to make "an amount of money that, at the time, I thought was a whole lot of money, and I'm going to do it working forty hours or less per week." But other students were allowed to critique the plans. One told him, "That's not realistic. In order to make that kind of money, you're going to have to work long hours. You're going to have to sacrifice your family."

Dave vowed to prove him wrong. Today, he's an author and an expert on time management and productivity. He works around thirty hours per week and takes every July and December off to vacation with his wife and kids. He didn't build a frenetic business for himself and then try to jam family time into interstitial moments. Instead, from the beginning, he built systems and structures around the time he planned to spend with them.

"The average person has mountains of inefficiency in their day, things that they put up with and they don't even realize it, because they've given themselves permission to work as long as it takes," he says. "When you give yourself permission to work long hours, to work continuously, you allow these little systemic, strategic inefficiencies to crop up all over the place."

Conversely, when you start with parameters like "I'm going to take all of July off," or "I'm going to finish work by six o'clock every night," it forces you to be creative in the systems you develop. You can spot inefficiencies—whether it's a slow-running computer or an awkward scheduling system—because you can't afford not to. And you're compelled to ask big-picture questions:

- Should I be doing this task at all?

- Could I delegate it to someone else, or stop doing it altogether?

- Where should I focus my effort in order to get the biggest return?

- If I were starting fresh today, would I still choose to invest in this project?

Like a poet deciding to write within the strictures of sonnet, you're leveraging positive constraints to make you sharper. Too many people embrace magical thinking when it comes to their calendars. They've said yes too often, which leaves them hoping everything will get done. Instead, there's a backlog, disappointed colleagues, and the never-ending feeling that you're behind.

"The most important thing is to get out of the habit of operating from a to-do list," Dave says. "Because a to-do list is like, 'Well, let's just fit it all in here.' You create a running list and there's no way to keep up with it."

People push Dave all the time to reveal his favorite productivity app. His answer invariably disappoints them: it's a calendar. "You want to determine what's most important, and then you schedule that the soonest in your calendar," he says. "Whatever is less important, you schedule it further out. Whatever is not important at all, you don't schedule it at all. You get rid of it. You delegate it. You say no to it. If you start operating from the calendar rather than a to-do list, you take back control over your day."

It's the productivity version of the quest for the perfect diet. Keto? Atkins? South Beach? Intermittent fasting? Actually, just eat less.

Almost no one likes the results of the short-termism we see around us: the relentless frenzy, the endless hamster wheel, the aggressive pursuit of goals that quite possibly aren't the right ones. But it takes strength to go against the prevailing culture. That's both internal strength, because we have to face down uncomfortable questions about who we are and what we really want, and external strength, because we have to deal with bosses and colleagues and clients who are still used to measuring productivity through face time and volume.

We have to be willing to make choices. And at a very basic level, we have to believe change is possible in the first place.

Years ago, I got to know David Allen, author of the famed productivity guide *Getting Things Done*. When I interviewed him for my book *Stand Out*, he shared an interesting insight. "You don't need time to have a good idea," he told me. "You need space. And you can't think appropriately if you don't have space in your head. It takes zero time to have an innovative idea or to make a decision, but if you don't have psychic space, those things are not necessarily impossible, but they're suboptimal."

It's not that you need to set aside hundreds of hours for long-term strategic thinking. You don't need to go on a monastic retreat or rent a farmhouse in Tuscany. But you do need mental space, and a little time, in order to think.

To become a better, sharper, and more strategic thinker, the first step is clearing away the nonessentials. But in a world of unceasing requests—and some amazing opportunities buried amid the dross—where do we even begin? That's what we turn to next.

Remember:

- Of course you're busy. But studies show that looking busy can also be a way of increasing your social status ("I'm important!") or a distraction from asking uncomfortable questions. Sometimes, we're unconsciously doing this to ourselves.

- Think about reframing what it means for people to be busy. The less we see it as "They're in demand," and the more we see it as "They don't even have control over their own schedules," the less appealing it will be.

- Schedule and set limits around your true priorities. Work could theoretically expand to fill all the time you have—so instead, put firm boundaries around it.

2

Saying No
(Even to Good Things)

The email came from a dear friend, one I hadn't seen for a while. "I'm sorry I've been missing in action recently," she wrote. But she had an offer in hand.

She was a member of "an invite-only group of entrepreneurs who are working in the social sector space. We're a cohort of designers, developers, digital strategists, and PR experts who come together each year to learn how to run our businesses better." Their upcoming annual meeting would take place in Grand Cayman— and they wanted me to be the featured guest. The lure was obvious: a chance to see my good friend, have interesting conversations with cool entrepreneurs, and land a free trip to a beach resort?

And yet. Something small tugged at me. I wanted to say yes— badly. But a part of me knew I should think *very carefully* before answering.

We're faced with situations like these all the time: invitations to professional events, or getting-to-know-you coffees, or catch-up calls, or requests to advise someone's friend or present at meetings or conferences. At first, it's flattering. Early in my career, I remember being thrilled when someone would reach out; it was validation that I was someone worth connecting with. I'd find a convenient time and location for them, and tromp across town to their local Starbucks. We'd kibitz for an hour (I never insisted on a clear agenda), and then I'd head home. But with walking and the subway and the usual delays, it may have taken forty-five minutes to get there and another forty-five to return. By that point, half the day was spent—and I wondered why I wasn't making as much progress, or earning as much money, as I wanted.

So I started getting more selective. I had to, or it would have been easy to let every day slip away, buffeted by other people's requests and schedules like a jellyfish against the waves. As my status (and, frankly, self-respect) increased, I made adjustments to my procedure:

- I wouldn't contort my schedule to fit theirs, but only agreed to times that were convenient for me.

- I requested that they come to a location near me, or we picked a time when I was already going to be in their neighborhood.

- I stopped agreeing to meet people "just because." In the early days of your career, when you don't know anyone, it's a fine starting point. But you have to become more selective, so I'd only meet with people who either had a relevant professional connection, or who seemed legitimately interesting.

Those modifications improved my schedule a bit. Over time, though, the quality of the requests kept improving—which was a good problem to have, but made them harder to say no to. Of course, I'd turn down the phone call with the random stranger. But what about the phone call with the friend of a friend? Or the invitation to be on someone's podcast and get more exposure? Or the offer to lead a webinar for a professional association that might have buyers in the room?

Eventually, I developed stricter criteria to deal with those situations too. *Only do podcasts when I have a book coming out. Only do webinars that are paid, unless it's for a worthy cause.* But like a Hydra growing new heads, the requests kept coming. Things I would have jumped at three years ago, or even the year prior, now gave me pause: *Do I have time to do that? How can I fit this in? Is it worth it?*

Which brought me to my friend's invitation to speak in Grand Cayman. Saying no is the ultimate weapon in the battle to become a long-term thinker—and it is a battle. "Yes" is easy in the moment, for so many reasons:

- We don't want to disappoint others or let them down. (*She was counting on me!*)

- We're worried about negative judgments. (*Will she think that I think I'm too good for her?*)

- We don't want to have hard conversations, and it's easier to avoid them. (*What will I even say?*)

- We like feeling important and that we're needed. (*They unanimously voted to invite me!*)

- We're plagued by FOMO: the fear of missing out. (*What if I find out later that everyone had the time of their lives? What if I miss the chance to become friends with the next Elon Musk?*)

For a long time, we can get away with it. Because let's be honest: early in our careers, not that many people are queued up to talk with us. There's margin available. But if you're doing things right, as you get more experienced, you become much more in demand. And what started out as a smart move—saying yes to all kinds of opportunities and seeing where they lead—becomes a major liability. We have to adjust and become far more selective.

People resist, of course, for all the reasons above. Your schedule doesn't become jam-packed overnight, so like the proverbial frog boiling to death in water, you barely notice the temperature rising. But eventually, for most professionals, our "yes" habit brings us the kind of chaotic, always-on schedule that we actually dread.

Most of us are desperate for more time to think, more serendipity, even a few moments to linger and enjoy a conversation or process an interaction. But we rarely get it. "Just look at your calendar," John Hagel, formerly of Deloitte's Center for the Edge think tank, told me. "How tightly scheduled are you? Have you got a breakfast meeting, meetings all day, then late-night meetings? There's not much chance for serendipity there unless a fire alarm goes off and you have to head into the street."

As the British scholar C. Northcote Parkinson noted, "Work expands so as to fill the time available for its completion."[1] The logic is inexorable: if you have free time in your calendar, unless you guard it vigilantly, it *will* get devoured.

Most of us don't want to live our lives that way. Yet we do— because the more successful we get, the more we're flooded with opportunity. And saying yes is, in the short term, the most expedient way to deal with it. We stuff our schedules to the gills and then wonder why we have no bandwidth, no ability to think beyond the next day or the next meeting.

So what can we do to make the hard decisions, say no, and create the conditions that enable the life we *actually* want?

Hell Yeah or No

One strategy comes from Derek Sivers, the music entrepreneur-turned-author mentioned in chapter 1, who eschewed the "out of control" busyness of so many professionals around him.

Years ago, he picked up a tip from a friend of his: "When deciding whether to do something, if you feel anything less than 'Wow! That would be amazing! Absolutely! Hell yeah!'—then say 'no.'"[2] This binary might sound extreme, and it is. As Sivers told me, "I'm too good at it. I say no to almost everything! Maybe to a fault." But as a result, he says, "my life is extremely simple and easy," and he spends most of every day focused on projects that are meaningful to him.

His mantra points to the crucial problem, though. Most experienced professionals are pretty good at saying no to terrible offers ("Could you copyedit my dissertation for free, by Thursday?"). We're also smart enough to snap up great offers when they come around ("How'd you like a promotion and a $50,000 raise?")

The issue is primarily with middling opportunities, those that have both good and bad aspects to them. It could be attending an event that seems tedious but that your friend invited you to. Or speaking for free when there might be useful contacts in the audience. Or doing an informational interview with someone's cousin's friend because you might need a favor from them one day.

That's where we get into trouble. And that's where "hell yeah or no" can save us, by forcing us to choose. Anything less than a nine out of ten on your excitement scale, or even a ten out of ten, becomes a "no."

So I summoned up my courage. It took me a little while to parse my concerns about the Grand Cayman trip. Eventually it became clear: I *could* make the trip work, theoretically. But my spring travel schedule was already so tightly packed, I knew I'd be exhausted and couldn't fully enjoy being there. And the organization was used to member-led presentations, which meant there wasn't a speaker budget. They could pay for my flight and hotel, but I'd be speaking pro bono. The chance to see my friend and take in some sun sounded appealing. But doing it when I was already exhausted, for no money? Maybe I could just meet up with her for dinner instead. I finally wrote back:

> Thank you so much for the incredibly kind invitation to speak to your group in Grand Cayman. It sounds like an incredibly interesting and fun opportunity, but I'll regretfully have to decline. After taking time to look at my schedule last night, I realized that I am going to be on the road almost continually from February through April, and really need to pace myself with travel next year, even to awesome places.
>
> My vow for this year is to get smarter about opportunity costs rather than saying yes to everything, even though this looks amazing. I truly appreciate you thinking of me, and if I can be helpful in another way (such as doing a webinar for your group), I'd be very glad to do so.

I winced when I hit the Send button. I hated to say no. But I did it.

Get Clear on Your North Star

Terry Rice was an experienced digital marketer; he'd worked for companies like Facebook, Adobe, and more. So it was no wonder his skills were in demand. "When I first started my consulting business," he told me, "a client offered me a $20,000-a-month retainer." That sounds like any new consultant's dream gig.

But not quite.

The new assignment "would have required me to commute from Brooklyn to Long Island every day," he recalls, which can take several hours, depending on traffic. "The main reason I started my company was to spend more time with my family. But with this opportunity, I would have rarely seen my daughter. Beyond that, I wasn't super enthused about the project I would have been working on. And given the time constraints, I wouldn't have been able to work on other projects I *was* passionate about."

Terry did something that more of us should: he identified the key values he wanted to use in evaluating opportunities. In his case, it wasn't money (if it were, he would have said yes instantly). Instead, he prioritized time with his family and the ability to work on interesting projects. That enabled him to cultivate the resolve necessary to stand firm. "The same company kept reaching out to me for a year," he says. "It was sometimes challenging to say no, especially during the slow months, but I'm glad I continued to turn down the opportunity."

Mary van de Wiel went through a similar exercise when a global advertising agency offered to purchase her Sydney, Australia–based branding and design firm. Her north star? Autonomy. "I talked to two boutique agencies that had already become part of their global acquisition program, and the clues I picked up? I wouldn't have the freedom I wanted. Plus, I was considering opening an office in New York, which I did in 2000, and knew that wouldn't be approved" by the larger agency. More than twenty years later, she knows it was the right move—and she eventually sold her firm to another bidder, on her own terms.

Sometimes the decisions we make aren't guided by our current state of affairs, but by who we want to become. That was the case for Tom Waterhouse.

It was fall 2007, and Tom, then an executive at a wealth management firm, had just been offered a dream position: chief operating officer of the Singapore office. "At the time, this was the job everyone in the company wanted," he recalls. "There were exciting plans for development and a big budget to pay for them. I loved Singapore, and had worked on several projects there. And I loved the people I would have been working with."

He'd be starting in February, but before that, he headed home to England to spend Christmas with his family. "One day my mother said to me, 'Everyone's really excited about you going to live in Singapore. Except you. Am I right?' She was, of course."

On January 3, his first day back after the holidays, Tom made what he describes as "one of the hardest phone calls I've ever had to make." He told the CEO in Singapore he had changed his mind. Tom still remembers the agonizing conversation. "It was like a breakup call. I told him it wasn't him, it was me. He put the phone down. He called me back fifteen minutes later and said, 'I don't understand. Did I do something wrong?'"

It wasn't any easier to tell the company's managing partner, who said Tom had "betrayed" the firm and that he couldn't trust him anymore. "He was true to his word," Tom says. "I spent over a year in purgatory before eventually being welcomed back into the fold."

When we say no, we're forced to ask: *Why put yourself through so much anguish? Am I an idiot to turn down such a coveted opportunity? Why risk incurring the wrath of friends and colleagues?*

But Tom was crystal clear. "I was forty-two and still dreamed of having a family and watching my children grow up around me," he says. "I have an adult son, but his mother and I separated when he was two, and he moved with her to another country. I knew that if I took the job in Singapore, my work would consume me and I would not be maximizing the chances of meeting the right person."

Tom—unlike Terry Rice—wasn't choosing to spend more time with his family. He didn't even have a wife and kids yet. But he knew that accepting the great opportunity in Singapore meant greatly diminishing the possibility of that ever occurring. He was making a bet.

In life, we just don't know what's going to happen or how things will play out. But if it's important enough, we have to try anyway.

Two years after Tom turned down the assignment, and "just as I was beginning to reconcile myself to the idea that my dream would never be realized," he met the woman who became his wife and the mother of their two children.

Decide What to Be Bad At

Let's be clear: no one likes to be bad at anything.

Sure, there are things we've never really studied ("I wouldn't even know where to start with electrical engineering"), or maybe even inabilities that have become part of our identity ("I'm terrible at sports"). But if we're talking about the core competencies of our field, no one ever wants to be bad. Or even mediocre. It's like the business equivalent of the "Lake Wobegon effect," in which all the children in town are purportedly above average.

That's the phenomenon Frances Frei and Anne Morriss tackled in their book *Uncommon Service*. I first got to know Frances, a Harvard Business School professor, and Anne, an entrepreneur, nearly a decade ago, when I interviewed them about the book for *Forbes*. Their focus was on customer service, especially in retail businesses, and they tried to understand why so few companies were outstanding, and so many were . . . meh.

The answer quickly became clear. The businesses didn't want to turn off any potential customers, so they tried to be everything to everyone. We all know that doesn't work, yet companies couldn't resist the urge to do the exact same things as everyone else. Led by smart and highly paid executives, they failed to execute on the most basic element of strategy: making choices. Meanwhile, it turned out that, paradoxically, the most successful companies were the ones who were unafraid to *choose what to be bad at.*

Every company would love to be great at A, B, and C all at once. But it doesn't work that way. If you're going to be great at anything, it comes at a price. The trade-off that most companies refused to make was accepting that in order to be great at something, you had to be willing to be bad at something else.

Every bank would love to stay open later. That's far more convenient for customers. So why don't they? It costs money, and no one wants to spend it. But one bank Frances and Anne profiled in their book, Commerce Bank, went all in. It offered service seven days a week, including staying open until 8 p.m. on weeknights. How did Commerce manage pay for it when no one else could?

It made the deliberate choice to offer *abysmal* deposit rates. Of course, if you asked customers, "Would you like to earn a pathetic amount of interest on your accounts?" the answer would be obvious: no. But for the particular customers this bank served, earning interest just wasn't that big of a concern. The ability for them to pop in after they finished work made much more of a difference in their daily lives.

As Frances and Anne note, "Choosing to be bad is your only shot at achieving greatness. And resisting it is a recipe for mediocrity."[3] In reading their book, replete with case studies of banks and airlines, I realized: the same principle applies in our own lives. Too often, we're afraid to make choices, to say no, and to close some doors so we might have room to open others.

The consequence, though often invisible to us, can be dire. It's cramming your calendar so full, you're constantly leaving one event early and getting to another one late. It's never truly making progress, because you're moving a million things an inch, instead of one thing a mile. And it's always being in "reaction mode," because you're so focused on what's coming at you that you never create your own agenda.

Saying yes to everything means being *average* at everything. Saying no, conversely, is what gives us the rare opportunity to be great. That certainly means letting some people down: no, I can't take the coffee with your cousin, or give the free talk, or look over your draft. And it likely means you need to be bad at some things. When I'm working on books or other long-term projects, I've made peace with the fact that my inbox is going to spiral out of control, and some people may be upset that my response time will be slow. But one way or another, we have to choose for ourselves if we want to accomplish anything at all.

Request Further Information

The next tool in saying no seems awfully counterintuitive: asking for more information about why they want to connect. After all, doesn't that just prolong the encounter? Requesting extra information, however, serves two powerful functions. First, it eliminates a certain percentage of requesters off the top (I'd estimate close to 25%), because some people are so disorganized that they simply won't follow up a second time.

Second, it enables you to make far better decisions about where, how, and how intensively you want to assist someone. The truth is, many people—both newbies in business and those who really should know better—are lazy or uninformed when it comes to networking. They heard from their college career counselor that it's a good idea to "ask people to coffee" and "pick their brain," and that's what they've been doing ever since.

They may have a hazy sense of why they want to speak with you (a friend recommended it for unclear reasons, or they saw your name in an alumni magazine or on LinkedIn), an inaccurate view of what you actually do, or unrealistic expectations of what you can provide ("Can you introduce me to Jeff Bezos?"). It would be great if they'd do the homework themselves, but typically they don't—which means that your job is protecting yourself from unwanted incursions into your calendar. Your time is precious, and you should allocate it accordingly.

Of course, you'll always want to help a good friend or a client, and you'll likely want to meet fascinating people or high-potential business leads. But for everyone else, the next time they suggest "hopping on a call" or "grabbing coffee" for no clear reason, it's useful—before agreeing to anything—to ask some questions to slow down the process, force them to think about what they want out of the encounter, and weed out people who aren't willing to make an effort.

For instance, you could say, "I'd love to see if I can be helpful. Can you tell me a bit more about what you'd like to discuss, and how I can be useful to you in particular?"

THIS REQUIRES THEM TO EXPLAIN:

- *What they'd like to talk about.* This eliminates the need for many conversations. They might want your advice about breaking into the public relations field, but it turns out that's not really what you do. This is your chance, before wasting an hour of your life, to explain that, unfortunately, you specialize in speechwriting and don't have useful information to share about the PR field. Or perhaps you're in the PR field and you've previously written an article about landing a job. Instead of meeting with them, you can instead send them the article as a resource.

- *How they think you can help.* Some people are hesitant to state their requests clearly—often, because they're outlandish and inappropriate. (I was once invited to someone's home for dinner, only to discover during the entrée course that her intention for the evening was to get me to invest in her film project. Dessert was very awkward.) Asking the question clearly helps prevent you from being ambushed, and sometimes enables you to redirect them to other resources. ("I don't have any connections at that company, but I suggest reading X book and Y blog.")

Perhaps most important, the extra step of requesting clarifying information forces people to make an effort, which most aren't willing to do. This ensures that the people you do connect with are the most motivated and diligent. They're the ones *worth* knowing.

Ask Yourself These Questions

We've all discovered by now that checklists work. If you're a pilot getting ready to embark on a trans-Atlantic flight, or a doctor prepping for surgery, checklists are an extraordinarily useful tool for preventing basic mistakes. Even if you're experienced and talented, we all have off days, and we're all subject to the occasional error. Asking the right questions, again and again, leads us to better results.

And yet, when it comes to most aspects of our professional lives, we don't use checklists. We don't even *have* checklists. Most of the time, we treat each request or opportunity as a unique problem to be examined and solved. As a result, we continually ask ourselves: Should I accept this invitation? Should I agree to write that article? Should I take that meeting?

We're wasting valuable cognitive capacity. Instead of treating everything as a yes-or-no vote we have to analyze, we should look at the big picture of where we want to go in our lives and how we actually want to spend our time.

Here are four questions I use with my executive coaching clients to help them think through requests, opportunities, and (seeming) obligations.

What Is the Total *Commitment?*

Everyone has a basic sense of how long something will take. The problem is, their estimate is often wildly inaccurate. It may sound innocuous to agree to present a free webinar, because it's only an hour long. But if you add up the planning calls, the messages back and forth, the run-through, and creating the slides, you're looking at three to four hours of work.

If you consistently underestimated the time or money needed on your company's work projects by a factor of four, you'd likely be out of a job. But we do it all the time in our own lives, and rarely even recognize the problem. For every request, think through each step—including hidden or unstated obligations—and create a rough estimate of what's actually involved. That alone may scare you into saying no.

What Is the Opportunity Cost?

It often feels like the choice at hand is simple: do the webinar or don't do it. But actually, it's a lot more complex.

The true choice is: do the webinar, or do anything else in the world that might take those same four hours of planning, prep, and execution. Maybe it's spending time with your family, or working out a few times a week, or taking piano lessons, or completing a long-term research project. The cost of *not* doing other things too often remains invisible. And in order to make good choices about our time, we need to bring it to the surface so that we can make meaningful, proactive choices, and not just accept whatever is offered to us.

If presenting the webinar is the very best use of those four hours, by all means, do it! After all, it might be a guest lecture for a prestigious university that can go on your résumé and increase your credibility. It might be for a C-suite audience that could hire your firm for multimillion-dollar contracts. It might be for a tiny, low-level audience—but one that lets you test your material before speaking at a major conference you can't afford to mess up. Any of those reasons might move this webinar to the front of the line.

But if you're saying yes because it's easier than saying no, it's probably time to reconsider your approach.

What's the Physical and Emotional Cost?

Technically, I could have fit in the trip to Grand Cayman. My friend was asking me six months out, and my calendar was open on those dates. But part of how I mustered up the courage to say no to this fun, interesting offer was considering the hidden physical cost. I already had business trips scheduled just before and after, so I'd be flying multiple weeks in a row. That meant jet lag, time away from home, needing to live out of a suitcase, less access to healthy food on the road, the stiff joints that accompany too much time in cramped airline seats, and—as I suffer from extreme motion sickness—multiple nauseating cab rides to and from the airport, on each end of the destination. Taking in the full picture of what a "yes" entailed helped me understand it wouldn't have been a good decision.

That's what happened to Manbir Kaur when she considered the emotional costs of what seemed like a great opportunity. More than a decade ago, as an executive in India, she received a plum job offer. "It was an amazing organization, with an awesome title, role, and pay," she recalls. But there was one catch. "The organization wanted me to work in a shift ending in the very late evening." As the mother of a school-age child, evenings were precious, one of the few times she'd get to spend with her young family. She ultimately turned the job down, but, she recalls, "it was a difficult thing to say no to, as a career woman who is ambitious."

The problem isn't saying no to terrible, boring opportunities: those are easy to dismiss. The problem—for Manbir, me, and most professionals—is knowing how to balance competing priorities when the offer is quite tempting. That's why it's so important to fully understand the hidden costs, including the physical and emotional, behind saying yes.

Would I Feel Bad in a Year If I Didn't Do This?

Some missed opportunities may sting in the moment, like looking at pictures of a friend's party online and seeing how much fun everyone had while you were stuck fulfilling another obligation. But odds are, in a few days the FOMO will subside. There'll be other parties, and while you may have missed a nice evening, it wasn't life-changing for anyone involved.

But some situations are different. And that's why, in evaluating what you choose to take on, it's important to ask yourself: in a year's time, if I didn't do this, how would I feel?

That was the question Su-Yen Wong asked herself a few years back. At the time, she was serving as CEO of a national leadership institute in Singapore. She had an ambitious vision for the organization and "my work there was not yet complete," she says. But then her father was diagnosed with stage four cancer. "Doctors said it was a matter of months," she recalls.

With any health crisis, there's uncertainty. But she realized that if her father did pass away in the near future, she would always regret not having the opportunity to spend more time with him. So, despite loving her job, she made the difficult decision to leave it. "My dad loved art and had built up a wonderful collection over the years," she says. "I ultimately spent four months going through his entire collection with him. It was a wonderful way for us to spend time together, and it brought him great joy up until the very end."

She even helped him create a legacy project. "As he had always focused on sharing his knowledge and collection with others, we even managed to push out two books during that time," she says. "He had the opportunity to see one in print and the second in digital proof before he passed on." Now a consultant and corporate board member, she looks back clearly on that time. "It was absolutely the right thing to do."

We don't know what the future holds, and our control over it is limited. But we can at least make better decisions if we broaden our time horizon and ask how we'd feel in a year (or five, or ten) as a result of our choices.

Clearing the brush is essential for long-term thinking: we need to stop spending time on ephemera, and set our own priorities. But the question remains: in a world of choices, what *should* we focus on?

Remember:

- Early in your career, saying yes is a great strategy, because you have plenty of time and you never know which connections will turn out to be valuable. But as you advance professionally and get busier, you have to start saying no more often.

- Most of us can identify great—or terrible—opportunities. It's the middling ones that are harder. Push yourself to say yes *only* to things you're excited about.

- Decide what to be bad at. You can't do it all. In order to be great at something, accept that you'll be terrible at something else. Refusing to make that choice leads to mediocrity.

- A great way to triage requests for your time is to ask people for more information. Many won't bother to follow up, and you'll quickly discover that others haven't done their homework properly, and you can weed out their requests.

- Four questions can help you determine whether something is worth doing:

  - What is the total time commitment?

  - What is the opportunity cost?

  - What's the physical and emotional cost?

  - Would I feel bad in a year if I didn't do this?

Focus Where It Counts

OOXOOO

Now that you've opened up room in your calendar (and your mind) to consider new possibilities, an important question emerges: What, exactly, should you be aiming toward? Playing the long game is great, but it's not always obvious what your goals should be.

How can we decide on the right ones? And once we do, where should we focus our limited time and energy for the best results?

That's what we'll turn to next.

3

Setting the Right Goals

The default in Western culture, almost always, is to optimize for money. It's why so many college grads without a clear plan migrate to law school or business school. In the absence of a compelling alternative, the thinking goes, you might as well make bank.

Of course, problems can arise. Companies that focus too obsessively on the bottom line may cut corners or engage in ethically questionable behavior. People that focus too intently on their bank account are susceptible to letting personal relationships suffer. None of that leads to good outcomes over the long term.

One possible alternative—a great one, if you feel clear about pursuing it—is to optimize for meaning. For some, the path to meaning is through working directly for a cause they care about, or perhaps the opportunity to maximize other interests, such as time spent with family or on a beloved hobby.

Others find meaning through their personal experiences. That's what happened for Rukiya Johnson when, in 2006, she learned that her brother, a college sophomore and community activist, had been murdered. In response, Rukiya decided to change careers and honor her brother's legacy by working in education, a cause he was passionate about. Today, she runs a program helping young students of color break into health care and STEM professions (science, technology, engineering, and mathematics). "I found my life purpose," she says. "It all clicked for me."

Rukiya's story is powerful and inspiring. But what if you're not quite sure what you're passionate about or what feels meaningful to you? What then?

Optimize for Interesting

I get messages from readers all the time—from recent grads to senior professionals—who are struggling with finding their "true passion," or their "real purpose," or what they're "meant to do." They believe, and have been told repeatedly by American culture, that each of us has a calling and it's our responsibility to find it. If we aren't sure what it is, or haven't located it yet, then there must be something wrong with us. As you can imagine, self-flagellation doesn't usually help the discovery process.

When you're still figuring out what feels meaningful, or if you're a Renaissance person drawn to many different things, I've found it's helpful to *optimize for interesting*. That's a lesson I learned when I launched my consulting business in 2006. One of the very first clients I landed was a woman running for lieutenant governor of Massachusetts. As a marketing and communications consultant, I had my work cut out for me: races for the job are notoriously tough because, frankly, most people don't care that much. Unlike with races for governor or senator or president, which can become epic PR battles, most of the public isn't really sure what a lieutenant governor does, besides hang out in case the governor gets sick or decides to resign. So in order to garner any attention at all, we had to think of something clever.

My candidate was an environmentalist, so we dreamed up a kayak tour around the state. She'd paddle down a few rivers (a hobby she enjoyed) and meet up with the local press to talk about her policy ideas. Unfortunately, the kayak tour wasn't enough to help her win office. But something significant did happen, at least for me. Through the kayak tour, I met Marion Stoddart, one of our guest stars on the tour. Marion was nearly eighty at the time, with short white hair, a lined face, and a kayak of her own. In the 1960s, she had led the successful cleanup of the Nashua River in Massachusetts, which was, at the time, one of the ten most polluted rivers in the country.

I was charmed and impressed, but after the race ended, I didn't think much about her. Until I got a call from a woman named Sue Edwards, who had volunteered on the campaign. "I can't stop thinking about Marion," she said. "Someone should make a movie about her life." I agreed. Her story was inspiring, and she'd be a charismatic subject. But who would do it?

I had some contacts in the documentary film world and offered to put Sue in touch with them. Over the next few weeks, she had sit-downs with three colleagues I'd suggested and began to wrap her arms around the filmmaking process. She came back to me with an offer: if she produced, would I direct it?

I'd never made a documentary film. But at its heart, I realized, it was storytelling: laying out the narrative arc and pulling together the images and dialogue to bring viewers along for the ride. As a former journalist, I knew I could figure it out. Most important, it would be interesting.

So I said yes.

I spent the next three years working closely with Sue and the team we assembled on the film, *Marion Stoddart: The Work of 1000*. We spent countless hours interviewing Marion, drilling down into her life, from how she was raised to which political organizing tactics she used to gain support for the river cleanup. But one story stands out. Marion was seventeen years old, and leaving home for college. As she approached the door, her mother gave her one last piece of advice. "Whenever you have a choice of what to do," she told Marion, "choose the more interesting path."

Yes, I thought, *that's exactly it*. When it comes to long-term thinking, we often assume we need to know the answers in advance. After all, how else can we plan? But no one is omniscient, and things frequently change along the way. It's not about setting a fixed goal at age twenty and methodically spending the rest of your life fulfilling it, whether it's still a good idea or not.

Wherever we are in our lives, we may not yet have identified something overtly meaningful that we want to do or are good at. But we all have things we're interested in and want to learn more about. A passion for photographing birds, for instance, may not seem to be particularly "meaningful." But if it's *interesting*, that curiosity spurs us toward mastery and may ultimately lead in useful directions, such as new personal and professional connections, a book deal, or a successful campaign to preserve local wetlands.

Some might question the premise of optimizing for interesting. Isn't that a pipe dream, or something only the wealthy can think about? "I have to stick with this job to pay off my student loans," they might say, or "I have a mortgage to think about." And that's fair enough—in the short term. But the whole premise of playing the long game is that we're not victims of circumstance. Our current reality isn't our fixed, eternal reality.

If there are things that pique your curiosity or fields you'd like to explore, you may not be able to quit your job today and go immerse yourself in them. In fact, very few of us could pull that off. But over time, with small, strategic steps, almost anything is possible.

But what if you've been working "heads down" for so long that you're not even sure what you find interesting anymore? What if you feel stuck or bored in your professional life, or feel confused, or just aren't sure where to start?

Evaluate What You're Already Doing

Often, the truest test of what's interesting to you is to look at how you're spending time right now. For instance, if your Instagram feed is littered with lovingly crafted close-ups of food, you might be a good candidate to one day become a food critic, or start a catering company, or head up branding for a food product company. If you can't get enough of podcasts and are always recommending new ones to your friends, maybe you could raise your hand and offer to launch one for your company, or seek a job working for a firm that produces them.

It's valuable to notice what catches and holds your attention. If you're someone who's interested in a lot of things, that's fantastic. Almost any topic is worth an hour of your life to read up on and learn more about. But don't rush to make your latest fascination the mission of your life until you've tested it out. Find ways to learn incrementally, such as setting up informational interviews with people who work in the field, or reading several books on the topic, or asking a friend if you can shadow them at work for a day. You can weed out fleeting interests and the lure of "shiny object syndrome" by seeing whether your curiosity sustains itself over time.

Additionally, look for overarching patterns in what attracts you. That's what Rebecca Zucker—the erstwhile banker from chapter 1 who realized she just wanted to live in Paris—did. She took on a hodgepodge of side gigs to make ends meet in the City of Light: "I taught English, helped people with business school applications, did interview prep for people doing banking interviews in London, presentation skills coaching, and other random consulting." Slowly, she discovered a pattern in her series of odd jobs: "I learned that I loved supporting other people to succeed."

When she finally returned to a corporate role, Rebecca moved into training and development. She recalls, "Everyone would come to my office to help them solve their work problems. I just listened and asked questions." Noticing what truly made her happy—and where others naturally gravitated to her—helped Rebecca realize she wanted to become an executive coach. A year later, she launched her own firm.

Constance Dierickx, who started her career as a stockbroker at Merrill Lynch, also followed her curiosity: why did people make such irrational decisions about their money? We all know the mantra: *buy low, sell high*. And yet smart people would consistently do the opposite, selling in a panic or becoming greedy when the market was obviously frothy. "I began spending hours every week in a bookstore, going back and forth between the decision science and psychology books," she told me.

She knew she enjoyed the deep relationships with her clients at the firm, but kept coming back to her interest in decision-making. Eventually, she hit upon a way to combine them: going back to school for a PhD in psychology. It wasn't an easy decision. "I was risking my family's financial well-being," Constance recalls, because Merrill paid well and being a full-time student definitely did not. But by taking clues from her emerging interest, she realized it was the right path forward. Today, she's a successful consultant and the author of a book about psychology and leadership.

Figuring out where your true interests lie may seem complicated. But often it's simply a matter of noticing how you're already spending your time—and, perhaps, reconnecting with what motivated you in the past.

Remember Why You Started

"I'm an artist," Sarah Feingold told me, "and I went to law school because I wanted to help artists like myself." But it didn't quite turn out that way. After getting her degree, she took a job at a small firm in upstate New York. She drafted motions, drew up contracts, and worked on real estate deals. She was learning a lot about the law, but she didn't feel satisfied. "At the firm, I wasn't representing artists and small businesses, and I wasn't practicing intellectual property law," she recalls. "I spoke with a law firm partner about this, and it was clear that nothing would change if my career was left up to anyone but me."

What did bring her joy, though, was making jewelry— necklaces, earrings, and rings—on the side. A few months earlier, she had started selling her creations on a new website called Etsy. Digging around the site one day, she had a revelation: "Etsy didn't have an in-house attorney, and my goal to help artists could come true if I worked for them."

Then one day, Etsy announced some new policies. Sarah had questions, and also some legal insights to share. Since the company was still small, she managed to get the CEO, Rob Kalin, on the phone. They had a short, positive chat, and then Sarah decided to press her luck. She booked a plane ticket to New York City to pitch for a job. It was a brazen move—she didn't even have an appointment—not to mention an impractical one. Most startups fail, and this tiny enterprise wasn't even selling a respectable B2B product. It was a craft emporium.

"I told him I was coming down for an interview," she recalls—and Kalin told her he was busy. But eventually her chutzpah persuaded him, and he agreed to fit her in. She made her case: "As a member of the Etsy community, I understood the community and their needs. I knew I could add value to the company and help it scale. I was uniquely positioned to work there." Even better, she could take work off his plate: "He mentioned some legal questions he had, and I told him I'd handle it."

Kalin hired her on the spot.

"At the time, people thought what I did was ridiculous," Sarah recalls. Why give up a safe and steady job? But safety and security weren't what had brought her to law. She'd studied it so she could help other artists: *that's* what was interesting to her, and she was willing to fight for it. "I moved to New York City and worked at Etsy for nine-plus years," Sarah says. She eventually helped to take it public, and the tiny online craft store where she first sold her jewelry is now a multibillion-dollar company.

When you're unsure of where your interests lie—or you feel like you used to know and have lost touch—go back to first principles and think about what inspired you at the beginning of your journey. Sometimes we just need to remember what got us started in the first place.

Forget What Others Think

Other times, we have a sense of what we'd like to pursue, but worry it's the wrong move. That was the case with T. J. Wagner, an army officer I met several years ago.

For a number of years, I've worked with the consulting firm Deloitte on a corporate social responsibility initiative it runs, the CORE Leadership Program, which helps military veterans on the cusp of transitioning back into civilian life think through their career goals, how to talk about their military experience, and more. I've delivered a keynote about professional reinvention more than two dozen times. But one of those evenings stands out.

It was late—nearly ten o'clock—and the crowd had dissipated. I was getting ready to leave as one last soldier rushed up: "Do you mind if I ask your advice?"

T. J. was clear on what he wanted to do, but that was the problem. "I'm just not sure it's a good idea," he told me. He was starting business school in the fall, but there were nine months until then. His dream was to go to sailing school, secure his skipper's license, and captain a ship in Greece and Croatia over the summer. He had major concerns, though. "I was afraid to go through with it because it would leave a significant gap on my résumé," he recalls.

Would this look like a ridiculous, hedonistic lark? Would potential employers judge him? Was he making a major mistake?

It was the end of a long night, and I'd talked to nearly fifty service members that evening, all bright, talented, and competent.

But T. J. immediately stood out because he had a unique vision. He was memorable, and that, I was convinced, could become his competitive advantage.

"Everyone wants to have an adventure like that," I told him. "They'll want to live vicariously through you, and it will make you an object of interest. Do it." So he did. T. J. and his best friend signed up for a sailing theory class in the Philippines, then a sailing school in Malaysia, then a skipper academy in Croatia. "We did extremely challenging yachting maneuvers and always needed to be ready," T. J. told me. "One night the instructors untied the five yachts from the raft, and woke us up screaming and yelling, 'The raft is collapsing!' I felt like I was back in the army." He passed his final exam with a perfect score.

He spent the summer skippering in the Mediterranean, which he describes as "the best job in the world." His adventures make for a compelling story—one that would make almost any recruiter pick his résumé out of a lineup and say, "That guy seems interesting. Let's bring him in."

But that's not all. The real advantage of optimizing for interesting isn't just that you can accumulate cool stories to tell at the bar. It's that pursuing interesting experiences opens up possibilities that otherwise may have been hidden or inaccessible.

Newly equipped with his sailing skills, T. J. joined the sailing club at his business school and, finding it in organizational disarray, promptly got himself elected president and recruited more than fifty members. His foray into sailing became a powerful networking lever, since it afforded him a natural opportunity to connect with his classmates, students on sailing teams at other business schools, and alumni who had been members of the club.

Sailing the Mediterranean definitely wasn't a conventional choice, but it was the right one for T. J. He distinguished himself by disregarding the conventional wisdom and carving a unique path. In playing by his own rules, T. J. didn't just become interesting: he became a beacon to others who longed for some of that magic in their own lives.

What Kind of Person Do You Want to Be?

Here's another great question to ask as you're figuring out which goals to pursue: what kind of person do you want to be?

It all started with *Hamilton*. My friend Alisa Cohn was obsessed with the musical by Lin-Manuel Miranda, eventually seeing it on Broadway eight times. One day she learned about another of Miranda's creations: Freestyle Love Supreme Academy, a course that teaches participants beatbox improv rap. "Without knowing much about it," Alisa recalls, "I said, 'Sign me up.'"

But it wasn't quite that easy. Classes were packed, so there was a waiting list. When she finally got accepted, she kept deferring, because the timing was never quite right: "I hemmed and hawed for almost a year." It wasn't just the schedule, though. Her fears rattled around in her head: "I'm going to look stupid, I'm not going to do well, I can't do this, everyone's going to laugh at me. I'm sure I had childhood flashbacks of being bullied or laughed at as a kid."

She forced herself to go to the first day of class, and walking into the room, filled primarily with men two decades her junior, she knew she was an outlier. "Half of the group had some, or even a lot of, experience," she says. "And I had literally zero experience. Most of them at least had an affinity for rap, which I totally didn't. I had learned rap from *Hamilton*."

She spent three hours "practicing and realizing I'm not very good at this." And then it was time for the evening's grand finale: "We have to stand around in a circle, and when your turn comes, you have to freestyle gibberish rap, on demand, right there in front of everybody. And I had to pass my first time. I literally couldn't do it. I was so self-conscious."

But then it hit her: "Part of my inspiration and my desire [to take the course] was overcoming my self-consciousness. I have creativity inside of me, and I want to unleash it. And I knew that this would help." On the next go-round that night, she mustered up her courage and chimed in. Eight weeks later, she performed her own freestyle improv rap onstage in front of sixty spectators as part of their graduation showcase. "I'm not saying I was good, because I wasn't that good," she says. "But I was good enough, and I got through it and everyone was very supportive."

Since the class ended, Alisa has kept up her rap efforts. She hired a friend to write a rap about her work as an executive coach for startups, and she recorded it and filmed a homebrew music video on her iPhone. ("Yo—comin' in hot with that rap charisma, it's your executive coach, and my name is Alisa!") Alisa isn't intending to become a rap star, and her video isn't necessarily going to land her new clients. But to her, the experience is about something bigger: "I think it is going to continue to lead me down the path of more creativity and being more unleashed, more unfettered, and less self-conscious."

There are a million reasons not to try something new, especially something outside our comfort zone. We can point to a litany of perfectly valid excuses. But the timing will never be exactly right, and there'll always be something more important that takes precedence—if we let it. Playing the long game means acknowledging we aren't already experts at everything, and that it's OK to sometimes look foolish in service of becoming the person we want to be.

Go to Extremes

So often in life, we take pains not to set ourselves up for disappointment. So we play it safe. If it doesn't seem practical, why even think about it? We dream of becoming a senior director or assistant VP—not the CEO.

Or we "think big" and plan how to land a gig for our band once a week at the neighborhood pub, instead of plotting how to hit the Billboard charts. The whole point of playing the long game is understanding that ridiculous goals are ridiculous *right now*—not forever. When we force ourselves to take our goals to extremes—*What would ultimate success look like?*—we can create an honest road map for ourselves. It might take five years, or ten, or twenty. But that time will pass anyway.

If a goal is worth pursuing, it's worth pursuing the version of it we actually want—not one that's watered down to protect our ego. Big goals on their own might feel paralyzing. How do you even start to write that novel? But big goals coupled with small, consistent efforts can be exactly the galvanizing force we need to achieve something powerful, especially in the face of overwhelming odds.

That's how it was for Luis Velasquez, who was working as a professor at Michigan State University when he received terrible news: he had brain cancer. Luis had no illusions about his situation. As a scientist, he knew exactly how dire his prospects were.

The weekend after receiving his diagnosis, he and his wife were in Chicago—by coincidence, the weekend of the Chicago

Marathon. "We stood at the finish line for several hours," he recalls. "We were standing so close and I remember being able to see the emotion in the runners' faces as they finished the race. Some of them were crying as they sprinted toward the finish line, while others were walking, obviously in pain. That's when I noticed that many of the runners had small signs on their shirts. I leaned in closer to get a better look and saw that the signs stated they were cancer survivors, domestic violence survivors, breast cancer survivors, brain tumor survivors, and so on."

Luis turned to his wife: "Next year, I want to run this marathon."

But after his surgery a short while later, Luis got a reality check. "I asked the doctor when he thought I could go back to work and start training for the marathon I was going to run," Luis recalls. "He said, 'Luis, you probably won't be a professor anymore, and it will take a long time for you to walk straight. I wouldn't be thinking of either of those right now.'"

Luis wouldn't listen, though. He renamed his daily physical therapy regimen "my marathon training." And, he says, "when I was given exercises, I would do them 10x, or sometimes 20x, the amount they prescribed." It wasn't an easy process. "I would get exhausted, I would get dizzy, I would get headaches."

Through his extraordinary effort, he regained his ability to walk straight. Next, it was time to run. "What really kept me going," he says, "was the thought of doing something that most people thought was nuts. Looking back, that was the biggest motivation—surprising people. And in the process, I would be getting my self-confidence back."

Many people, suffering from the effects of brain surgery, would have heeded the doctor's admonition: *You're lucky to be alive. Forget about the marathon.* But to Luis, his goal made all the difference: "Running, at that time, became the only thing that was giving me a sense of winning."

Exactly one year after his brain surgery, Luis crossed the finish line of the Chicago Marathon. "I remember looking back, perhaps the last mile, and I couldn't contain my happiness," he recalls. "I started to cry, and I cried all the way to the finish line. Just a year ago, I was there, wondering if I would be alive the next year."

In the years since, Luis has continued running marathons, and even became an ultramarathoner, clocking one-hundred-mile races. To overcome an extreme enemy—his health challenges—he created an extreme goal for himself. And day by day, through his unglamorous regimen of physical therapy and strengthening exercises, he made his vision real.

Recovering from a brain tumor certainly has higher stakes than, say, tackling a high-profile new project at work (though that can spark its own fears and anxieties). But we can all learn something important from Luis's example.

He could have listened to the voices of caution around him ("Forget the marathon") to avoid setting himself up for disappointment. But instead, he recognized the huge motivational power of having an extreme goal. When you're working toward something meaningful, that goal can carry you through the tedium of the small, everyday steps needed to accomplish it. When it comes to optimizing for interesting, what's really interesting isn't a goal that feels manageable. It's working toward a goal that's remarkable.

Across the country, Marie, a young jazz musician, was doing just that.

How Do You Get to Carnegie Hall?

We've all heard the joke about how to get to the legendary music venue Carnegie Hall: "Practice!"

It turns out, though, there's actually another way. Carnegie Hall lets individuals or organizations rent out an auditorium for private events. When Marie Incontrera learned about the possibility, she was thrilled. "There are different levels of social proof that you can get in your music career," she says. "Carnegie Hall is the top." Even if you rented it yourself, "it still means that you've reached a certain level in your career. You were able to fill the seats, you were able to pay for it."

The hall rental fee? Just under $6,000. Marie recalls, "I was like, 'Cool, I can do that. That's not that bad.'"

Unfortunately, though, that was only the start. "Then it was $15,000 in union expenses," she says. "All the labor, the tickets, the stagehands, and anything else that you wanted to do in the space was more money. If you wanted to have props on the stage, you had to hire a prop master. If you wanted to have a microphone, it was extra money. If you wanted to have video, you had to pay recording fees." At that point, she still hadn't even gotten to the line item to pay her own musicians in the band.

All in all, the expenses came to $40,000. That's a significant fee for anyone. But for Marie, who was scraping by with her cat in a one-room studio in the far reaches of Brooklyn, it seemed impossible: "The budget for the one night was almost three times what I had made the previous year." But her band was excited by the prospect, and she'd already started raising small amounts of money to fund the concert. She decided that somehow, the shocking enormity of the price tag aside, she'd make it work.

She spent months writing grants and reaching out to individual donors, and she even used funds that she earned from a nascent side gig as a social media consultant. Through the fundraising process, she says, "There were really high moments of wonderful victories and, 'Oh my God, this is going to make my life better.' Then there were moments of, 'Oh no, this is going to fail. I'm going to be paying this off for the rest of my life, or I'm going to go into bankruptcy, or I'm going to lose my apartment.'"

But she didn't. Using this extreme goal as a motivator, she scraped until the last minute and raised the funds. "I think that to this day, it was the hardest thing I've ever done," she says. Years later, the experience still impacts her. Playing at Carnegie Hall, she says, "is still something that I can point to and say, 'I've done this,' and people just pay attention. They pay so much more attention to me when they hear that."

Too often, we tend to look at where we are right now, and say, "Where can I go from here?" But that's asking the wrong question. If you start with your present situation, you're limiting yourself out of the gate to what seems attainable. Sometimes, as Marie and Luis showed, we need to choose extreme goals—even ones that sound impossible. Because nothing else is quite as interesting, or as galvanizing.

When we make the choice to optimize for interesting, we're investing in our future selves. We don't know where it will lead, and that's the whole point. Playing the long game means preparing ourselves for an uncertain future, where, because of the effort we've invested over time, we're ready to take full advantage of the opportunities life presents. (For Marie, who has subsequently built her side gig into a successful social media consultancy, that's turned into writing both a musical and a TV pilot.)

Over the course of this chapter, you may have identified numerous possible goals for yourself, or at least areas that seem potentially interesting. But how can you determine which are the most promising? Which should you actually prioritize? And could there be a way to test them out before going all in?

Fortunately, there is.

Remember:

- The default in our culture is to optimize for money and choose a lucrative career. Often, the only other alternative that gets talked about is optimizing for meaning—but not everyone is clear yet on what's meaningful to them.

- One possibility is to "optimize for interesting" and follow your curiosity. Ask yourself:

  - What am I already doing that I enjoy? Look at how you already spend your time voluntarily, which is a strong indicator of genuine interest.

  - Why did I start on this path? Think about your original motivations for pursuing your field or interests, and reconnect with them.

  - How can I tune out others' judgments? Not every experience or path has to be linear. Just because something isn't the established path doesn't mean it's the wrong one.

  - What kind of person do I want to be? Identify experiences that will help you grow into that.

  - How can I think bigger? Don't be constrained by what's possible now. Think about where you'd like to be in the future.

4

Time to Explore

It was late December 2015 in New York City. Everywhere you looked, sparkling white lights glinted across tree branches, and elaborate Christmas displays filled the storefront windows of Fifth Avenue. But I was huddled in bed with a cough and a fever, wondering what I was doing.

That year, I'd given seventy-four talks to promote my book *Stand Out*, most of them in other cities. Once or even twice a week, I'd clamber into a taxi and head to the airport, eat questionable late-night meals from whatever restaurant was still open, and then do it all over again. As I tossed and turned in my febrile state, I wondered: *Why did I bother to live in New York, one of the most expensive cities in the world, if I was hardly ever home?*

The new year was just days away, so for my resolution I decided I would do at least one "uniquely New York" activity per week. Going to see a movie, no matter how nice or fancy the venue, was out—you could do that anywhere. Going to see a Broadway show, on the other hand, was very much in. I'd lived in the city for more than a year, and during that time had seen exactly one show, when an out-of-town visitor requested we go.

And that's how I found myself bustling past the tree at Rocke-feller Center with Bruce Lazarus and his son, heading to see *Fun Home* on Broadway. I'd met Bruce a few weeks prior, when we spoke at the same conference. He was the head of Samuel French, a company that licenses plays and musicals. *Fun Home* was one of theirs, and he had an extra ticket. He invited me to join, and I jumped at the chance.

I'd never been a particular fan of Broadway. I grew up listening to pop music, not show tunes, and my small-town school didn't have a theater department. My mom had tried to expose me to culture, but her efforts, including a trip to see the traveling pro-duction of *Cats* in Raleigh, North Carolina, had left me mystified. *Why didn't I understand what was going on?!* (Hint: the show has no plot.)

But *Fun Home* was different—a beautiful gut punch of a show. The next morning, I woke up early and headed to a coffee shop near my house. I was consumed with a thought I'd never had be-fore: *I have to write my own musical.* I had no idea how—I liter-ally Googled "how to write a musical"—but I vowed I was going to learn.

20% Time

When Google went public in 2004, it popularized an exciting concept: 20% time. "We encourage our employees, in addition to their regular projects, to spend 20% of their time working on what they think will most benefit Google," founders Sergey Brin and Larry Page wrote in their IPO letter.[1] "This empowers them to be more creative and innovative. Many of our significant advances have happened in this manner." Indeed, Google News and Gmail were products of 20% time experimentation. (The concept was originally created by the company 3M, which allowed employees "15% time" to innovate, leading to creations including the Post-it note.)

There's something compelling about the idea of cordoning off time to experiment and see where your passions take you. In the previous chapter, we talked about strategies to identify your interests. But there's a wide gulf between being intrigued by a topic and actually making it a core part of your life and career. That's where 20% time comes in, because it gives you permission to explore your interest and see what works while the stakes are relatively low.

Of course, devoting even 20% of your time to exploration isn't easy. People are busy, and not everyone is up for extra work on top of their already demanding day jobs. As former Yahoo CEO Marissa Mayer, who was previously a longtime Googler, has noted, "The dirty little secret of Google's 20% time [is that] it's really 120% time." In other words, these special projects are "stuff that you've got to do beyond your regular job."[2]

One estimate from a few years ago said that only 10% of Googlers make use of 20% time.[3] That's not especially surprising in a busy work environment—even one that theoretically encourages the practice. Most professionals are so focused on fulfilling their day-to-day responsibilities, they never make the effort to embrace 20% time. But that creates an opening for you.

For any of us, there are certain times and circumstances when we might not have the bandwidth to take on discretionary projects. But if you push when you're able and you do the hard work of carving out 20% time, you're often in rare company—and your experience has the potential to be transformative.

That's what happened for Adam Ruxton, the head of marketing for a robotics project at X, formerly known as Google X, the company's "moon shot factory," which has launched initiatives around everything from delivery drones to autonomous cars. A native of Ireland, Adam started at Google's Dublin office in 2011. By the end of his first year, he was already volunteering part of his 20% time to help the London office think through how to introduce Google apps in different European countries.

He saw it as a form of professional development. "The marketing program at Google is very interdisciplinary," he says, "so we're encouraged to go to different teams. You're hearing things about how they work, different products, different users, and you bring all that knowledge to your next role." You start by asking questions, he says. Perhaps you book a coffee with someone on another team that's interesting to you. "You ask about what's important, what's happening, what they need help with, or what they need more brainpower on."

You develop a hypothesis about how you can help, because coming in and demanding to be handed an interesting project is a recipe for disaster. The reaction, he says, is, "Oh, you're going to be work." Instead, make it clear that you're going to take work off their plate. As Adam notes, "If you go and say, 'Hey, I read ten articles. I found this deck. I see these three things. I have an idea that this is where you need to go in the next couple of months or years. Have you thought about these five things? I'd be happy to spend a few hours on it a week'—it's hard [for them] to say no." That's your opening, he says. "And then, if there's a fit, naturally over time, you get invited to more meetings, you're in the circle a little bit more, you get entrusted with things."

That's how Adam first got involved with X. A colleague had landed a job working on the self-driving car project, and Adam was desperate to get involved. "When I say 'an opportunity arose,'" he recalls, "it's a very fancy way of saying I begged: *Could I help?* I was extremely interested in the future of mobility and what they were doing. It was exciting." He spent several months volunteering on a research project to better understand how customers learn about and adopt new technologies. Adam is pretty sure his work didn't lead to anything earth-shattering. "In these 20% roles, you're not in a position to direct much, or make big sweeping moves or anything," he says. "It's more of, 'Hey, I'll fill gaps. I'll help where I can.'"

But that's OK. Besides his initial 20% project with the London team, he's tackled myriad other interesting side projects. He worked with a colleague, using a "small team prototype budget" to create a fully immersive, 360-degree virtual experience to help businesses better understand the online experience of their customers. That project took off and has been used by thousands of customers internationally.

Regardless of each project's outcome, Adam kept volunteering and meeting new people. And not long after, it was announced that Google X would rebrand to X. Of course, the team would need marketing help to do it—and the person doing the hiring was someone Adam had just worked with. As a result, he landed the opportunity of a lifetime: to work in the heart of Alphabet's moon shot factory and help lead its rebranding.

The truth is, it's challenging to carve out 20% time—even if you work at the company that popularized the concept. You have to make the extra effort, fight against other pressures on your schedule, and create your own openings. But the rewards of experimenting strategically are worth it. "You can make most of the opportunities you want for yourself, if you're deliberate and proactive about it," Adam says.

As you build new skills and connections, and stress-test whether the concepts that intrigue you hold up under pressure, keep asking those core questions. *Do I still find it fascinating after exploring it further? Do other people seem interested too? Do I see openings where I can make a contribution?*

Building Your Life Portfolio

"In risk management and banking, they talk about certainty versus impact," says Jonathan Brill, the innovation strategist we heard from in the introduction. "If you're investing in a bond, it's a very certain investment, so you don't have a huge return. But if you're investing in SpaceX in 2001, it better have a massive return" to make up for the risk.

A company that only makes moon shot bets could succeed fantastically—or go out of business if none of them happened to pan out. (That's why X, where Adam Ruxton works, is only one arm of Alphabet.) The same is true for individuals.

A few of us put everything on the line. Elon Musk, the founder of SpaceX and the CEO of Tesla, comes to mind. Buoyed by an unshakable faith, he plowed most of the $180 million fortune he accumulated at PayPal into these two companies—to the point where, by his own admission, he ran out of cash in late 2009.[4] Since then, he's recovered just fine, becoming one of the world's richest men. But his bet-it-all strategy isn't an amazing recipe for success; it's just as easy to imagine thousands of would-be Musks doubling down only to lose everything. Their stories aren't told in *Fortune* or the *Financial Times*.

Most of us, though, take the opposite tack. We know the risks are enormous, so we play it safe. We go to a college or grad school our parents recommend, get a steady job, and follow the script. In Jonathan's analogy, it's like buying a bond: you know you're not going to become a billionaire, but you're also unlikely to go bankrupt. Of course, there are drawbacks here, too. The point of life, one hopes, isn't just to "not go bankrupt."

What if there was a third way, one that could balance the risks of Musk-like innovation with the security we need to feel safe and provide for our families?

At its heart, that's what 20% time provides.

Jonathan has applied this principle in his own life. Every year, he focuses on landing what he calls "heartbeat income," a baseline of money that will pay the mortgage and give him the minimum standard of living that he needs. But beyond that, he's actively looking for opportunity. "Then I figure out, where can I spend 20% of my time on very high-risk activities?" he asks.

With the right opportunity, the payoff can be immense. He found one in 2015, with the World's Fair in Milan, which was centered around food, an area of interest he wanted to research. There was a lot of red tape regarding the event, Jonathan discovered. Larger players in the industry stayed away, leaving an opening for him. He took a lead role in the early planning for the U.S. pavilion, reckoning that if things went well, "I can get a 10x return on my time." Most important, no matter what happened, he knew he'd find ways to benefit.

"I wanted to learn more about government policy, I wanted to learn more about the food space, and I wanted to network in that space," he says. "So even if this wasn't successful, this was likely to result in new business development and some unique learnings that, as a small-business person, I could gain about how the highest levels of government actually work." That would have been enough to make the experience worthwhile. But sometimes, when you put yourself in the right position, new opportunities emerge that you couldn't have predicted. "I did several million dollars of business as a result of that learning," Jonathan says, in the form of high-level consulting for a food and beverage company.

Not every experiment is going to pay off—and we don't know in advance which ones will. Some of Adam's 20% projects at Alphabet went nowhere, but one of them led to his dream job. Jonathan landed a huge contract from his World's Fair volunteer efforts, but they just as easily could have been for naught. The key idea here is taking chances, being willing to accept that some things won't work, and knowing that others will—but might seem stupid or pointless or ineffective along the way. "You've got to be willing to ride out a period of loss" to do 20% time, Jonathan says. "Short-term pain is inevitable." After all, if it were a perfectly safe bet, it would be a bond, not SpaceX. There'd be zero chance of an outsize reward.

Here's the bottom line: you should never bet more than you can afford to lose. That's why it's only 20%. But you do need to bet something, because otherwise, you can expect a lifetime of doing the same thing over and over again. Some people suddenly become willing to experiment when things have gone badly. Their dreams have been shattered, and their backs are against the wall. That's the wrong time, Jonathan says, and way too late. It takes time to develop your side opportunities: "Do it when you're strong, not when you're weak."

But with steady, consistent effort, even 20% can lead to disproportionate—and life-changing—returns.

My Year of "Uniquely New York" Activities

The year 2016 started with a vengeance. It wasn't just attending the Broadway show with my friend Bruce. I started researching neighborhoods and creating lists of fun things to do. Each week, I'd knock a new milestone off my list, solo or with a friend. I took a walking tour of Borough Park, a traditional Hasidic neighborhood. I visited the Museum of the Moving Image in Queens. I finagled an invitation to the taping of a not-yet-released TV show. I attended an event at the historic Yale Club, took an underwater bicycling class (apparently you burn more calories when submerged), and saw Barbra Streisand in box seats at the Barclays Center.

Every single activity was a learning experience and a good story to tell later on, whether it was amazing or not. (The opera version of *Macbeth* staged inside a chocolate factory sounded like such a good idea—until we arrived and discovered it was unheated. In November.) All of them, ultimately, were "little bets," microexperiments to see what resonated. Some were perfect just the once; I enjoyed my pole dancing fitness class, but don't need to do it again.

Other activities stuck, though. Inspired by a friend, I signed up for a stand-up comedy class, something I'd never done before. I eventually spent three months of my life taking weekly classes and performed in comedy clubs around Manhattan.

And I couldn't quite shake that post–*Fun Home* conviction that, somehow, I needed to start writing musical theater. My Google search wasn't that helpful. *How many songs should be in a musical? How should you structure it? Who could I get to write the music to match my lyrics?* I did my best. In a creative flurry, I spent several consecutive weekends creating the book and lyrics for a musical about entrepreneurship—sort of a *How to Succeed in Business without Really Trying* for the internet era. I suspected it probably wasn't that great, but didn't know what to do.

Then, a month later, I attended a dinner at a conference. It was random seating, and I found myself next to a successful musical theater writer. When I told him my story, he had one emphatic instruction: "You have to join the BMI Workshop!" Since 1961, BMI, the music publishing company, has run a workshop to train the next generation of musical theater composers and lyricists. It's considered the premier training program in the country, and for good reason: if you can make it through the rigorous application process, you'll enjoy *two years* of completely free instruction. The program received a special Tony Award in 2007 for its contribution to musical theater.

I cobbled together my lyrics and submitted my application— and was summarily rejected. I didn't even make it past the first round. I was disappointed, of course. But I was playing a longer game. *These people haven't seen the last of me*, I thought.

Carving Out Time for Opportunity

Taking on a 20% project sounds appealing. Who wouldn't like to finally learn Italian, or take piano lessons, or get cracking on that novel? It's what we've been saying for years that we actually *want* to be doing.

That's part of why, at the outset of this book, we talked about how to clear your calendar—to create more white space and understand that busyness isn't the mark of success. On the contrary, it's something to be avoided at all costs. We need time, even just a bit of it, to experiment, because the rewards can be so vast. You can make important business connections that lead to lucrative contracts, like

Jonathan did. Or, like Adam, you can showcase your skills to potential new hiring managers.

Even if you have no idea what your ultimate goal is professionally, embracing 20% time is still a good idea. That's what university professor Marlena Corcoran discovered. She and her husband moved to Munich twenty years ago when he was offered a teaching position. Shortly after her arrival, she received an email message asking if she'd be willing to volunteer on Brown University's alumni interviewing program, as area chair for Poland. Of course, Munich is not in Poland. But, she recalls, "the alum who contacted me was desperate" because it was so hard to connect with Polish applicants. Marlena, whose grandfather was born in Poland, "immediately understood why: you cannot cold call people in a formerly communist country." She adjusted the procedures and ended up reaching 100% of applicants from Poland that year.

Impressed with her success, Brown rapidly promoted her— still as a volunteer—to area chair for Eastern Europe, and then regional director for Europe, Africa, and the Middle East. "I had only one idea, but it was a good one," she recalls. "Forget the model for New Jersey [where] alum meets candidate in Starbucks. Instead of geography, pair applicants with alums who, no matter their location, have an affinity for the region—ethnicity, college major, willingness to learn, anything."

Her work was enormously fulfilling, especially because while she'd been adjunct teaching in Germany, she had struggled to land a permanent position. After winning an award, Marlena realized she could turn "my volunteer experience into my life work" by starting a business to help international students apply to elite US colleges. Marlena discovered her new direction organically

through her 20% time, and as her husband put it, "You now have
the teaching job everyone dreams of."

Some of us may already have a general sense of where we want
to go professionally, but just aren't sure of the path to get there.
20% time can help with that, too.

Becky Last had spent fifteen years in the tourism industry, but
had pivoted away from it in recent years and discovered she missed
it. She wasn't quite sure how to break in again, so she decided to
volunteer for a year with Australian Volunteers International (the
country's equivalent of the Peace Corps) to assist the Ministry of
Tourism in the small Pacific island nation of Vanuatu. "My friends
thought it was a terrible idea," she recalls, "but my gut disagreed."
This would be her opportunity to reconnect with a field she loved
and help others in the process.

But things didn't go quite as planned. Not too long into her tenure, she recalls, "a Category 5 cyclone ripped through the country
and destroyed the sector literally overnight." Most of the ministry
staff members, like everyone else in the country, were consumed
with family and community obligations. So Becky stepped up. "As
one of the few ministry staff with the bandwidth to continue working, I took on responsibility for the damages/loss analysis and writing a sector recovery plan," she says. She'd never done anything like
it before. "It was vastly senior to my scope of work, and outside my
private sector experience," she says. But she figured it out.

Immersing herself in Vanuatu's recovery, Becky worked closely
with the World Bank and other donor organizations, "two of
which took me on as a tourism consultant in the aftermath, with
the ministry sponsoring a further two years in Vanuatu," she says.
Today, Becky is a full-time staffer with the World Bank Group,

heading a portfolio of tourism development projects in the Pacific. She knew she wanted to reconnect with the tourism industry somehow, but the exact path was murky. By following her gut and leveraging her volunteer time, she developed coveted new skills and opened up an opportunity she never could have predicted.

The other reason 20% time is so valuable is that new efforts often take a while to transform into a source of income. Christina Ryan, now a nonprofit leader in Australia, was committed to fighting for social justice issues from the get-go. "I was involved in women's rights for a long time and sat on various national working groups representing disabled women's organizations," she recalls. For well over fifteen years, it was a volunteer activity.

Through that process, Christina became a recognized expert in her field, including traveling to the United Nations in New York as part of Australia's delegation to negotiate crucial women's rights agreements. "I was called on by many other organizations to take the gender/disability role on working groups and delegations," she says. Eventually she started to get paid. "My voluntary work [became] my professional expertise for the next decade," she says.

Sometimes, though, the best reason to pursue 20% time is simply because you want to fulfill a dream.

Make It Real

There are a million reasons why you might put off a goal that, at least theoretically, you want to accomplish. For Petra Kolber, an author and speaker, that audacious dream was learning—at age fifty-six—to become a DJ. Partly, it was simple procrastination. Partly, it was self-doubt: Could she really pull it off? And partly, it was the desire to do things *just right*. "If I was going to DJ, I wanted to do it well," she says. "I wasn't going to show up and do a mediocre job. I wanted to blow people away."

Of course, that's an awfully high bar when you're trying something you've never done before. We all face obstacles and internal barriers—and if want to master 20% time and get good at accomplishing our stated goals, we need to learn how to outsmart ourselves. Here are six ways to do it.

Get the Right Support

When Petra announced her plans to learn to DJ, one musically minded friend bought her a device that allowed her to mix and preview music. "I'll get you ready for this," he pledged.

"If you don't have that accountability partner," Petra says, "and if you haven't stated [your goal] out loud, written it down, and declared it somehow, when things get tough, that's when we quit. Because we see everyone else's success seeming so easy." She knew the antidote was support from trusted friends.

Hire a Coach

Petra had her friend to help advise her. But not all of us know someone who's an expert in the area we'd like to break into. There's plenty we can learn on the internet, but one of the best ways to fast-track our learning is to hire a coach. That's what Zach Braiker did. The CEO of a marketing and innovation consulting firm, Zach had always had a passion for literature. "It was always my favorite class in high school and college, and the teachers inspired me to live my best life," he recalls. But as a busy

CEO, he didn't have time to read as much as he might like—and even if he did, it wasn't clear who would be willing to discuss it with him.

But the Covid-19 pandemic made something very clear to him. "In the quarantine, the grind of daily routines, anxiety, working from home, higher stress, constant changes, and seeing people less really took its toll on me," he says. "I knew I needed to do what I loved, and too often I made compromises—focusing on the urgent over the important." He wasn't going to let that happen anymore. "I made a choice, an investment, to put what I love first and foremost, and to be held accountable to pursue what I love," he says.

Zach hired a literature coach. It might not occur to many people that such a thing exists. But Zach figured since there are so many online tutors, surely someone would agree to have chats about books with him. So he explored a variety of platforms and ultimately hired an English-speaking PhD student in literature from a Mexican university. Every Friday night, they meet for an hour to discuss a short story they've agreed to read that week, by authors ranging from Salman Rushdie to Raymond Carver, and Ursula Le Guin to Jhumpa Lahiri.

"First, we discuss whether we, at a gut level, enjoyed reading the piece and why," Zach says. "We take turns. Then we usually pick a character and start to analyze her motivations, what surprised us, the choices she makes. Then we discuss how the story was built from a craft perspective, and what choices did the author make to bring the story to life. We look at language, the pacing, use of metaphor."

Some might ask why he bothers. Reading is great, sure—but why go so far as to pay for a coach? "It brings me energy," Zach says. "It cultivates my curiosity—for real. It's refreshing to spend time in someone else's world for a while. I also really enjoy hearing my tutor's perspectives. She's so sharp and always finds ways of looking at a narrative I would never have thought of—and the fact that she's international also means she brings a whole new way of looking." He's clear on the value: "I want more literature in my life, and therefore, I won't let this go."

Zach's strategy is applicable in many fields. After my application to BMI's musical theater workshop was rejected, I decided to try again the next year. But I wasn't going to make the same mistake twice, so I hired a coach. Through a friend, I connected to Christiana Cole, a lyricist and composer in the workshop's advanced class, who analyzed my submissions, offered edits and suggestions, and helped me fine-tune my application. Thanks to Christiana's help, I was accepted into the program the following year.

Give Yourself a Deadline

It's always easy to put something off until tomorrow. There'll be plenty of time in the future, when you're less busy.

But you're never less busy.

What almost all of us need, in order to get moving and take action, is a deadline. And that's exactly what Petra Kolber was handed at the launch party for her book, *The Perfection Detox*. Onstage, the interviewer asked what could have been a throwaway question: "What's next for you, Petra?" She hadn't planned an announcement, but—on the spot—she mentioned her dream of DJing. Later that evening, a friend, who ran one of the largest fitness events in North America, approached her. It wasn't really a request so much as a command: "A year from now, next August, you'll DJ our VIP party."

It didn't seem quite real at the time, Petra recalls. "I'm like, OK, sure. A year away, whatever!" But as the year progressed, Petra began to realize the enormity of what she'd committed to: running the after-party for a high-profile, six-hundred-person event. "There's nothing more terrifying than seeing an empty dance floor," she says. "And you know that you're going to be responsible for filling that dance floor. The stakes were high, and the potential for public humiliation was real, had it not worked."

With the deadline in sight, she stopped dithering. Learning to DJ was now serious business—so she drilled down on her training.

Keep Your Learning Going

Petra's showcase at the VIP fitness event turned out to be a smash hit. "I knew what song they needed. I knew what would fill the floor," she says. For many of us—especially if we're not planning to turn our 20% project into a full-time gig—it'd be easy to let up once the big event is over. But after you've put in all the work, that would be a mistake. You have to put structures in place to solidify your learning and keep growing.

So when Petra visited a rooftop bar across the street from her New York City apartment, she saw an opportunity. She asked the bartender, "Would you ever want a DJ?" He told her the hotel had just launched a new event series, Rosé on the Rooftop, and to her astonishment, they asked her to perform the following week. "It was amazing," she says. "I got to meet people in my neighborhood. I got to enter into a different style of DJing, where I'm not rocking the room. I'm now the background to their experience over cocktails. So it was just a great way for me to practice things with a lower risk."

She's used the opportunity to take musical chances. "I've mixed things, and sometimes I went from *Hamilton* into P. Diddy. I was like, 'This sounds like a beat. Let me just try it.'" Every time, she's learning and improving. And if something doesn't quite work, it's not the end of the world.

Inspired by her experience learning to DJ, Petra decided to buck expectations and take another big chance two years later. She fulfilled a long-standing dream to spend a year traveling around the world while working as a "digital nomad."

Win—Even If You Lose

Here's the ultimate way to de-risk your 20% time: make sure that even if you lose, you still win. That was what Jonathan Brill did when he took on the World's Fair project, knowing that regardless of the outcome, he'd build new skills and make valuable connections. It's useful to identify the minimum benefit you'll get out of a given situation or opportunity, even if nothing else breaks your way. Perhaps it's exposing you to a new industry, or helping you make connections in a region, or enabling you to learn a new piece of software, or helping you practice valuable skills like public speaking. If that minimal outcome alone sounds intriguing, then the project is likely a good bet. Any additional benefit—job offers, or consulting opportunities, or other things we can't control—is simply the cherry on top.

Think in Decades

There's a well-known saying: we overestimate what we can accomplish in a day, and underestimate what we can accomplish in a year. That's true, and it's even more true that we radically underestimate what we can accomplish in a decade. Just like with an investment in the stock market, when you invest your time in 20% projects, the power of compound interest is dramatic. What at first seems small and meaningless ultimately enables you to put massive distance between you and your competitors.

Theater lore says it takes seven years, on average, for a show to reach Broadway. You have to write the show, of course, and get it in good enough shape that you feel proud of it. Then you need to raise funding for successive workshop productions, where you continue to revise and hopefully interest an actual producer. They'll raise even more capital for an off-Broadway showcase (like *Hamilton*, which started at the Public Theater in New York City), or perhaps an out-of-town tryout (many shows get fine-tuned in cities like Boston or Chicago or San Diego before heading to Broadway). Finally, it's time to head to the Great White Way, which costs in the neighborhood of $4 million for a play and $15 million or more for a musical. It was a slow and laborious process even before Covid wreaked havoc on the industry.

So you have to be patient.

That's why, in 2016, when I was first struck with the thought that I needed to write a musical, I created a ten-year plan to land one on Broadway. I knew I needed a long runway—time to learn the craft, hone my skills, make the necessary connections, and move the project forward. I don't know if I'll really write a show that makes it to Broadway for the 2026 season. It's possible that my priorities will change, or the external world will.

But what I do know is I'm infinitely further along than I would have been if I hadn't developed and started acting on a long-range plan. In the years since, I've gone from rank novice to a competent musical theater lyricist, with a pedigree from one of the world's best training programs. Knowing I'd need to build relationships with producers, I also started investing in Broadway and other theatrical productions in 2017, alongside my friend Alisa Cohn. We've now invested in three Broadway shows (including a multiple Tony winner) and an Australia/New Zealand touring production. In the process, we've met and befriended nearly two dozen producers. None of that guarantees success toward my goal, but knowing the right people makes me more educated about the process, and certainly doesn't hurt.

Too many professionals berate themselves because they don't yet know their ultimate vision. That's fine—really, who does? Things change all the time, and part of success lies in capturing emergent opportunities that we couldn't have predicted. The gift of 20% time, especially when we think in decades, is that even if we ultimately change plans or decide on a different course, the small steps we take now compound over time, and give us more options in the future.

With 20% time, we can experiment with no consequences— only learning. But an important question emerges: Once we identify a promising idea or concept, where do we go next? How do we get started? How do we turn it into something real and lasting?

Remember:

- No one is going to hand you development opportunities on a platter. You need to seek them out proactively.

- Think about devoting 20% of your time to explore new areas. It's enough time to get a meaningful sense of whether you enjoy something and whether it has the potential to be impactful, but not so much of an investment that you'd be destroyed if it didn't work out.

- The best time to test out new ideas is when you're in a strong position—not when you're in a weakened one and are desperate to find the "next thing." Start planning now!

- Ask yourself: "How can I win, even if I lose?" In other words, even if the bet you place with your 20% time doesn't work out, are there other benefits you can derive that are still valuable (for instance, building your network or gaining new skills)?

- Think in decades. If everyone else is thinking a few months or a few years out, you can create a massive competitive advantage for yourself if you're willing to go slow—and perhaps ride out short-term losses or setbacks—in order to achieve much bigger things over a period of ten years or more.

5

Think in Waves

You can't do it all at once—that much is obvious. But a trap that many talented professionals fall into is they pick one activity or type of activity that they're good at, and they simply keep doing it forever. It feels productive, and to a certain extent, it is.

But eventually, they get frustrated: Why isn't their career moving faster? Why do they feel like they've hit a plateau? Often, it's because they've overplayed their strength and ignored areas where they're weak, or they feel uninterested, or in which they're afraid to take a chance.

For instance, it's easy for a writer to just crank out book after book. He knows the process of researching and putting thoughts to paper, so he does more of it, assuming that's the winning formula. Instead, he'd have far more success if he took the time to *market* each book by doing podcast interviews, webinars, speeches, and guest articles. That seems obvious, but so many of us are caught in our own version of that mistake.

The secret is understanding where you are in the process, and making strategic choices about when to go all in and when to shift focus. We'll talk about how to do that next, but I've developed a free self-assessment to help you think this through. You can access it at https://dorieclark.com/toolkit.

Strategically Overindex

It's often the case that you can make the most progress by focusing disproportionately on one key goal, rather than spreading yourself thin across several. So it's important to ask yourself: "Where can I get the greatest return on investment right now, and how can I do as much of it as possible?" It's easy to set yourself apart when you overindex.

That was my strategy when I started attending the ideas conference Renaissance Weekend. Not to be confused with medieval-themed Renaissance faires, Renaissance Weekend was founded in 1981 by Phil and Linda Lader as a convivial gathering of their friends over New Year's. As their professional fortunes rose—Phil became the ambassador to the United Kingdom[1] during the Clinton administration—the event grew. Eventually it attracted more than one thousand high-level attendees, as well as breathless media speculation about the off-the-record meetings that President Clinton and other luminaries regularly attended. As a politics-obsessed teenager growing up in small-town North Carolina, even I heard about it, and I wanted in. I wasn't sure how I was going to get there—my parents were far from connected—but I set my intention.

More than a decade later, I still didn't know anyone who could get me in. It said clearly on the website: "invitation only." But I decided to try anyway. I wrote a heartfelt letter, explaining my credentials (not many at age twenty-nine) and my long-standing desire to attend, and asking if they'd admit me. A couple of months later, to my amazement, a card arrived in the mail. There wasn't an explanation or a cover letter; it was just a listing of the next four gatherings and a registration form. I was only two years into running my business, and money was still tight. But I was more than a little fearful that they'd rescind my invitation—and I decided it would be harder for them to do so if they'd already accepted my money. So I checked the boxes and, sight unseen, signed up for every single upcoming gathering, to the tune of well over $10,000, if you include hotel and airfare.

It wasn't quite a leap of faith, because that phrase implies risk and uncertainty. I had done my research well enough to know that building a high-level network of interesting people was my top priority at the time, and that this was the right place to do it.

The first event, sure enough, wasn't easy. There seemed to be a crowd of regulars, and I didn't know any of them. I felt overloaded, meeting hundreds of new people at once and trying to intuit the norms of this new community. But there was no backing out: I'd registered for three more. And over the course of the next year, I became comfortable in that environment. By my third event, I felt like the mayor, greeting old friends and making introductions. I don't go nearly as often now, but the benefits of that early overindexing linger every time I see someone I met during that period, or get introduced to someone they brought along.

The same principle was at play in early 2012, when I began writing for *Forbes*. By that point, I'd started writing for *Harvard Business Review*, which sharply limits how much it publishes: only about five new articles per day online, and far fewer in the print magazine. I knew that content creation would be critical to building my brand and my business—but I'd need to do a lot more of it. I needed another venue to share my ideas.

I started by making a list of more than two dozen media outlets—national papers, regional dailies, cable television, even some prominent foreign press—and finding out whether they accepted online articles from people, like me, who weren't their employees. I reached out to every plausible publication, offering to write for free . . . and only three wrote back. I responded with story ideas and pitches, but two publications quickly dropped off, and I never heard from them again. But one, *Forbes*, was just ramping up its roster of contributors and wanted to know if I could come on board immediately. Within ten days, I had published my first piece.

I had a choice: write for *Forbes* occasionally for free, or commit to writing at least five articles per month and become a paid contributor. I opted for the latter, not because I was desperate for the money (it was modest, to say the least), but because it served to focus me. With a contract in hand, I had to prioritize content creation, which was my stated goal anyway.

Over the next few years, I wrote more than 250 articles for *Forbes*—sometimes as many as ten in a month—and leveraged it to dramatically grow my name recognition, my following, and my network. (It helped that for most pieces I interviewed an author or corporate leader.) Some people in similar positions might say, "I'm busy, so why don't I do the bare minimum necessary to say I write for *Forbes*?" And depending on where you are in your career, that might be the right strategy. But sometimes, if the opportunity in front of you lines up perfectly with your goals, you might want to strategically overinvest.

Heads Up, Heads Down

Another framework that's been useful to me as I've learned to navigate responsibilities and determine where to focus is *heads-up and heads-down*. I first heard it articulated by Jared Kleinert, an Atlanta-based entrepreneur and an editor of *2 Billion Under 20: How Millennials Are Breaking Down Age Barriers and Changing the World*.

I was interviewing Jared for my book *Entrepreneurial You*, and he started talking about "shiny object syndrome" and how hard it is for many entrepreneurs—and frankly, many people—to stop themselves from chasing the next big thing. It's the ultimate in short-term thinking, because jumping from one thing to another never allows any idea, no matter how wonderful, the time it needs to flourish. "It's really hard to identify what the number one thing you should be working on is, because you can only really figure that out in hindsight," Jared told me. You might have a reasonably successful project, "but is that the real thing? Do I stay and figure it out? Do I try other things and see if they work?"

Jared told me there's no shame in trying other things, "but only if you're in a heads-up mode. If you're in a heads-down mode, and you've identified what's working, then stick to it."

According to Jared, there's a time for each mode, and it's essential to know which one you should be in. "You can be in a heads-up mode, where you look for new opportunities, or you can be in a heads-down mode, just executing and focusing." Confusing the two—constantly scouting for something better when you should be doubling down on what's working, or doubling down on something when you haven't sufficiently vetted the possibilities—only leads to heartache.

In the years since, I've adopted Jared's credo. I'll set aside blocks of time—typically three to six months—in an explicit heads-up or heads-down mode. In the former, I'll merrily set up dinners, calls, and meetings to network, and accept interviews and podcast invitations to promote my work. But all that changes when heads-down mode rolls around. I'll turn down all but the most urgent requests, and spend hours at a time immersed in deep work on projects like developing a new online course or writing a book. This approach enables me to focus when needed, cluster similar tasks (to lessen the cognitive load of multitasking), and stay refreshed by changing up my routines.

In exercise, you're not supposed to lift weights every day; your muscles need time to recover, heal, and grow back stronger. You're more effective when you work in cycles than if you slog forward, repeating the same tasks every·day. Switching between heads-up and heads-down enables you to leverage the power of focus to your advantage. And on a broader level, that's the idea behind a concept I developed called Career Waves.

Thinking in Waves

When it comes to making smart choices about where to allocate your time, I've come to believe in *thinking in waves*. There are four key Career Waves in becoming a recognized expert in your field: Learning, Creating, Connecting, and Reaping. Like ocean tides, we need to learn to ride each wave, and then transition into the next. Trying to hold on to a wave for too long leads to frustration and stagnation. But when you can absorb the lessons of each and then gracefully shift, it enables you to keep growing, developing, and moving forward.

Learning

In the mid-2000s, I was the executive director of a bicycling advocacy nonprofit. I like to think it was noble work: we pushed for more bike lanes, bike racks on buses, the development of rail-trail corridors, and more. It was also the most high-stress job I'd ever held. Saying that felt strange—my previous role had been running press for a presidential campaign, where I worked seven days a week and was chronically sleep-deprived. But at the nonprofit, I was almost single-handedly responsible for our finances, and the burden of keeping myself and our two staffers employed was on me. My predecessor had landed a big government grant a few years prior, but it expired just as he left. I had to raise $150,000 a year, almost from scratch, or we'd go out of business.

For two years, I did it, and even managed to double the size of our membership base. But partway through my tenure, a thought struck me: I wasn't just running a nonprofit—I was running a six-figure business. And I realized I could do the same for myself. I had never thought about becoming an entrepreneur before. Many people think going into business for yourself is risky. But for me, earning $36,000 a year and waking at least twice a week in a sweat about the future of our little organization, starting my own consulting practice seemed lucrative in comparison. If the bar was $3,000 a month, I was sure I could find a way to beat that.

I just didn't know where to start. I had plenty of skills: I'd been a reporter and a political campaign operative; I could write and speak well. But I'd never had to land business or win a client. Some of what I was learning at the nonprofit was transferable—simple web design and databases and the like. But the rest of entrepreneurship was a black box. So I decided to learn.

For a full year, I committed myself to studying. I made a list of all the things I didn't know that I suspected I needed to. On Saturdays, I took daylong courses at the local adult education center on things like writing a business plan, designing better PowerPoint slides, and basic bookkeeping. I convinced my employer to pay—it wasn't much—because the skills would help me at the nonprofit. But even an $89 course felt like a lot at the time.

And I became my local library's best patron, picking up an armful of books with each visit. I'd spend evenings reading through classics of business literature, from Michael Gerber's *The E-Myth Revisited* to Keith Ferrazzi's *Never Eat Alone* to Jim Collins's *Good to Great*. I'd note what was referenced in the footnotes of one book, then follow the trail backward to see what else I should be reading and build up my cultural literacy.

I knew I had to immerse myself in learning before I built my business, because if I didn't, who would take me seriously? That wasn't a lack of self-esteem—it was a fact. I didn't have an MBA or a PhD in business; I had never even worked in a corporation. I was a philosophy major as an undergrad and had a graduate degree in theology. Those are solid credentials, but not necessarily a compelling reason for corporate executives to listen to my counsel. Given my background and approach, I suspected I'd probably break a few conventions once I started my business—and that's a great way to differentiate yourself. But you have to do it consciously, and understand what convention looks like in the first place. Otherwise, it's just ignorance.

Part of playing the long game is understanding that you can't always immediately jump into the ring. Moving slow may feel like wasting time. But every moment you spend understanding the nature of the game, and how it works, makes you stronger once you do get in.

Of course, there are limits. I once had to stage an intervention with a friend who complained constantly that her business wasn't growing the way she wanted it to. After a cursory round of questions, the reason became clear: instead of doing things that might actually generate clients, like asking for referrals or writing articles to generate publicity, she kept signing up for new courses and certifications. She had spent untold sums of money searching for the training that would magically enable business to drop into her lap. But learning doesn't generate income on its own. It's one important step in the journey, but it's only the first wave. Once you've familiarized yourself with the basic frameworks and ideas in your field, and have begun formulating your own perspective, it's time to create and share your ideas.

Creating

It started with inviting a few friends over. It was 2016, and Kara Cutruzzula had left her job as a magazine editor to become a freelance journalist. "Not having coworkers is great in some respects," she recalls, but she found it a little lonely. So once a month, she'd hold a party. She called it a "Brass Ring Summit," and she'd invite some friends to her apartment to catch up and kibitz. But Kara wanted her gatherings to be *useful*, so she had folks go around in a circle and share tips about products or services they loved, things they could offer, or things they were looking for (advice, consulting gigs, a new roommate). Kara would take the minutes and share them afterward, and eventually someone suggested: Why not turn them into a newsletter?

When writing is your day job, the idea of starting an unpaid newsletter may sound like a busman's holiday. But Kara suspected the regular writing practice could help her hone her literary voice and stay sharp as a writer. And it could serve as an antidote to the up-and-down nature of being a freelancer. "You're dependent on other people to set deadlines and give you assignments," she says, "and this felt like something that was totally in my control. So even if I had no other assignments, it felt like I was producing something."

She started the *Brass Ring Daily* with a subscriber base of thirty: the invite list for her monthly house parties. Almost every weekday for the past few years, she's released a newsletter. Her reader list has grown significantly (it now numbers more than four thousand), but it's still a relatively small audience, and the newsletter doesn't directly generate any income. So why does she bother?

It turns out that the newsletter has a hidden benefit that she didn't realize when she launched it several years ago. Some of the editors she works with have subscribed, and "it's become a way for me to get more work, because they see my name in their inbox every single day," she says. By sharing articles she's written, or simply ones she's found interesting, she helps editors get a sense of the topics where she excels. "It's almost in a subliminal way—they know I'm around, and they see other things I'm working on and that I'm available [for assignments]."

In her biggest coup, a book editor cold emailed her. As Kara recalls, the editor said, "I'm working on a motivational journal, and I kept thinking about all the things that you write about in *Brass Ring Daily*. And then I thought to myself, 'Why don't I just see if Kara wants to write it?'" Kara signed the deal for her first book, called *Do It for Yourself*. Thanks to the newsletter, "it felt like she already knew my work. It was perfectly aligned."

Learning your craft is an essential first step, but if you want people to recognize you and the unique contribution you can make, at a certain point, you have to begin the second wave: Creating. You've absorbed others' perspectives and ideas, and have learned enough to evaluate them. Some ideas will resonate, and others will seem flat-out wrong, and you'll stir and sift them into your own point of view. Creating is how you can make a contribution to your field and attract like-minded people to you and your business.

Creating content and sharing your ideas can be a small step, like with Kara and her thirty initial subscribers. But it's powerful nonetheless, because it gives others—like the book editor who approached Kara—a way to discover you. Writing is one method for sharing your ideas, but it's not the only one; you can give speeches, or conduct webinars, or host a podcast, or create online video tutorials. The key is to make yourself "findable" by the people you'd most like to do business with.

That involves just a little bit of bravery. Maybe it's putting a link to your email newsletter in the bio of articles you write, as Kara does, or applying to present at a conference, or posting an article you wrote on the company intranet. Creating and sharing your ideas is a crucial part of the wave, and so is what comes next: playing on a bigger stage and leveling up your connections.

Connecting

As Kara's example shows, your reach can grow over time if you're consistent. But especially in the early days, it can be challenging to keep up the momentum. The first month is fun and novel, and enthusiasm can push you through months two, three, and four.

But what happens when you're six months in, and still talking to thirty people? Even if you've reached sixty or one hundred, you may begin to wonder: *Is all this effort worth it?* That's especially true if you're working in an area where you don't have much expertise or have doubts about your abilities. What can get you through—both by growing your audience and by helping you obtain the support and encouragement to keep going—is the third wave: Connecting. That's how it worked for Albert DiBernardo.

Al had spent more than forty years as an engineer and was working as the executive vice president at a major New York City firm when he announced his plan to step down once he turned sixty-five. He wasn't entirely sure what his next move would be, but he knew he didn't want a traditional retirement of sitting on the beach.

And that's when he logged in to Facebook. He saw a post announcing that a friend had just become a certified coach—a career Al didn't even know existed. But he was intrigued. "I took the train out to Newark, I took him to lunch, and I go, 'What's with coaching?' I was immediately drawn to it. He sat there and he explained the whole thing to me, and then I got that 'aha,' that epiphany."

Over the years, the part of Al's work that he'd enjoyed the most was advising younger leaders on how to develop their skills—and this was a chance to do it full time. He jumped into the Learning wave with abandon, joining my Recognized Expert program as well as other trainings and certifications, from health and nutritional coaching to emotional intelligence. "I went through this phase and paved lower Broadway with coaching certifications and degrees," he jokes.

But unlike my friend who wouldn't stop taking classes as a way to avoid building her business, Al didn't stop there. The trainings taught him methodologies to complement his intuitive sense of how to coach others. But the most important part of joining those communities, he says, was the connections he made. It was the connection with his friend in Newark, after all, that showed him the path to coaching in the first place. And as he progressed in his exploration of coaching, his new relationships kept him going.

He knew what could happen otherwise: "I saw enough people retire from the [engineering] profession. All those quasi-relationships fall away, because they were just situational." He'd seen others spiral into depression and loss of meaning when they left their jobs. Instead, he developed a raft of new friends and colleagues. "I was being fueled by the new relationships that I was getting. It was like a miracle drug for me."

Al didn't yet know how to be a coach or how to build a practice, but he surrounded himself with people he could learn from. "Just jump into communities of people," he says, "and you might not even know who your like-minded people are at this time, but you'll likely find someone within that community who [qualifies]. If you wait until you know, you'll never get there." It could be a learning community, like the courses Al joined. It could be meet-ups or professional associations or industry conferences. There are plenty of ways to do it. But if you're hoping to establish yourself in a given field, making an effort to get to know that world is key.

If you're a sworn introvert or lone wolf, connecting with others may seem frivolous—a needless diversion from your "real work." And you can get away with ignoring it for a while. But eventually, having a tiny network becomes a roadblock. You won't be exposed to new ideas (Al never would have discovered coaching if he hadn't stumbled upon his friend's announcement). Your ideas won't get the traction they deserve (because there's no one to amplify them). You'll be in the dark when it comes to pricing or other sensitive topics (because strangers don't disclose that—only friends and close colleagues do). And you won't get the opportunities you'd otherwise qualify for (because you need someone to suggest you, but you're not on anyone's radar).

Taking the time to connect with others and immerse yourself in new communities, as Al's example shows, can be a powerful way to set yourself up for success. Within a year of launching his retirement coaching business, he'd reached six figures in revenue.

As with everything in life, there's always the possibility of having too much of a good thing. One colleague I know is a sensational networker, who seems to know everyone and is constantly making connections. That's a great skill and a wonderful asset. But it's almost the only thing he does. He spends so much time making connections that he neglects almost every other part of his business, and his limited revenue reflects that. Thinking in waves means you can't focus exclusively on the parts of the process you enjoy. You have to keep moving and growing.

Reaping

Now you're in the final wave: Reaping. It wasn't easy getting here. You started out not knowing anything. You had to immerse yourself and learn—an especially humbling experience for midcareer or senior professionals who are used to being excellent at what they do. But you did it.

You began creating and sharing your ideas, and honestly, in the early days, they probably weren't very good. You look back now with a twinge of embarrassment. But you had to start somewhere, and you did.

You got to know people over time—colleagues, clients, industry leaders. You built relationships based on mutual respect and trust.

They referred business to you, and you did the same. You built a name for yourself, and over time, a career.

You surfed those waves, and now it's time for the fourth wave: Reaping. This is where it gets fun.

You've achieved a degree of mastery in what you do. You're confident; you know you can help people and make a difference. By now, the world agrees with you. The rewards—financial, reputational—are starting to become evident.

This is also where it becomes dangerous.

It was the late 1970s, and Marshall Goldsmith was a young college professor. One day, his mentor, an organizational behavior consultant named Paul Hersey, found himself double-booked. "He says, 'Can you do what I do?'" Marshall recalls. "I said, 'I don't know.' He said, 'I'll pay you $1,000 for a day.'" At the time, Marshall was making $15,000 a year, so for that price, he decided to figure it out. Before long, he was raking in six figures.

But Hersey was concerned. Not that Marshall wasn't good—he was. And not that the clients weren't pleased—they were. But as Marshall's mentor, Hersey had other things on his mind. "One day he called me," Marshall recalls, "and he said, 'You're *too* successful. You're making too much money, and you're never going to be who you could be. This is not bad. You have happy customers. You're doing a good job and you'll do OK, but you'll never be the person that you could be. You're not writing. You're not thinking. You're not investing in your future. You're just running around like a chicken with your head cut off, selling days.' And I have to say, for eight years he was right. I didn't change."

Marshall, deservedly, was reaping the rewards that came with being excellent at his craft. Earning a lot of money pays for mortgages, college, health care, savings—all important and worthwhile goals. But Hersey, in his warning, identified a crucial problem: Marshall hadn't sufficiently immersed himself in the Creating phase. Hersey believed Marshall should develop his own unique intellectual property that could distinguish him in the marketplace.

"It's very hard, when things are going well, to challenge yourself," Marshall says. "You're making a nice living. You have a house, maybe a mortgage, and comfort. And if you're not careful, the years pass very quickly and that's it. You don't want to look back on your life and experience regret."

Eventually he began to turn his attention to creating and sharing his own ideas more widely. Not everything hit; some books did better than others. But a few, like his bestsellers *Triggers* and *What Got You Here Won't Get You There*, have become classics in the field and helped established him as the number one executive coach of all time.[2]

It's crucial to realize: Reaping isn't a final destination. And by the time he'd reached his late sixties, Marshall felt it viscerally. "You can't ever be happy in life with a thing that used to be," he says. "[People will say] 'I used to be the CEO, I used to be the football star.' And what happens is, when the profession disappears, our identity disappears. We have no identity." Reaping has an expiration date: you have to create something new and start again.

Around the time he was grappling with these thoughts, he attended a workshop called "Design the Life You Love," which was organized by Ayse Birsel, a noted industrial designer who was named one of *Fast Company*'s 100 Most Creative People in 2017. She asked participants to write a list of their heroes, and Marshall wrote down his professional mentors: Hersey; Frances Hesselbein, the former CEO of Girl Scouts of the USA; and Peter Drucker, the famed management thinker. "They never charged me money,"

Marshall recalls. "They were always nice to me. They were kind. I was nobody, they were big deals, yet they were being nice to me." Ayse's advice to him was crisp and clear: "Be like them."

Before the workshop was over, he'd hatched a plan: he'd identify fifteen up-and-coming executive coaches and offer to mentor them and "teach them everything I know." The response to his concept was so overwhelming—he received more than seventeen thousand applications—he decided to expand the initiative, now known as Marshall Goldsmith 100 Coaches, or MG100. (I joined the community in the summer of 2017.) Through the program, he's intent on creating a culture of giving back. Reflecting on Hersey and his other mentors, he says, "The same way they helped me, my job is to help others." Indeed, the only rule of MG100 is that one day, "when we get old," we'll each create our own pay-it-forward initiatives.

Of course, Marshall gets something important out of his involvement as well. He's seen firsthand among colleagues and clients that telling tales about your past glory without learning or doing anything new is a recipe for depression: "You can't just go from being a CEO to playing crappy golf with old men at the country club, while eating chicken salad sandwiches and discussing gallbladder surgery," he says. MG100, in many ways, is the antidote: "It's really focused on achieving meaning for me now."

Marshall Goldsmith became the biggest name in his field: a multimillionaire, a bestselling author, a member of the Thinkers50 Hall of Fame, and a friend of CEOs and celebrities. You could excuse him, now in his early seventies, if he wanted to coast. But he refuses. As the Bible (and Bob Dylan) famously said, there is a time to reap. But it doesn't go on forever. The most successful people enjoy their success, then recognize: it's time to move on and learn something new.

"Right now, I'm working on a project where I have fifty people and we talk every weekend," Marshall says. "We're developing a whole new coaching process based on what [former Ford CEO] Alan Mulally taught me. I would say I would not have learned any of these things if [MG100] hadn't happened. So this has really been instrumental in reshaping my career, and reinventing myself again."

No matter how good you are, you can't win any game by doing the same thing all the time. You could be amazing at shooting three-pointers in basketball, but sometimes you have to play defense or sink a free throw. We all have strengths, but too many of us overplay them, and then get bitter when we don't get the results we want or expect. Playing the long game means understanding where you are in the game and what skill is necessary to deploy at what point. When you learn to think in waves, you'll choose your tool to suit the moment, and ensure that you don't stop and don't stagnate. That's how you win.

And now that we're focused on the right things, it's time to think about leverage. How can we double down on what's working to elicit even more-dramatic results in our lives?

Remember:

- To get more done, alternate between heads-up and heads-down modes. During the former, you're actively seeking connections and exploring new possibilities. During the latter, it's time to focus and execute.

- You can't do it all—at least, not all at once. Instead, follow the Career Waves, in which you sequence between:

  - **Learning.** Study your field so you become knowledgeable.

- **Creating.** Now that you have experience, give back by creating and sharing what you've learned.

- **Connecting.** Begin leveling up your connections with others in your field, so you can learn from them and contribute as part of the community.

- **Reaping.** You're at the top of your field, and it's time to enjoy the benefits of your hard work.

- Remember: don't stop learning. Soon, it'll be time to start the cycle over again so you don't stagnate.

6

Strategic Leverage

We've all been there. You get to the end of an exhausting day and look back on the past eight or ten or twelve hours. You were certainly busy, racing from meeting to meeting and answering emails in every spare moment. But you wonder: *What did I actually accomplish?*

So often, our days begin to bleed together. We can keep up—barely—if everything goes right and there are no traffic delays or dropped calls or jammed printers. But keeping our heads above water certainly isn't the same thing as accomplishing our long-term goals.

I wanted to get strategic about my life. But first, I needed data—where was my time actually going, anyway? Time tracking isn't fun. It's boring and meticulous, and marking down your life in fifteen-minute increments takes discipline. But in February 2018 (I deliberately picked the shortest month possible), I decided to do it.

My friend Laura Vanderkam is a productivity expert, and I downloaded a time-tracking spreadsheet from her website. I left it open on my desktop so that anytime I returned to my computer from a break, it would be the first thing I'd see. I had to constantly remind myself to fill in the blanks (2–2:30 p.m. client calls; 2:30–3 p.m. email; 3–4:30 p.m. write article). But for a full month I made myself do it, and what I learned was truly shocking.

If we want to use our time strategically, to accomplish the things we claim are important to us, we have to learn to ask ourselves different questions. The first is: *How can I leverage time that otherwise would be wasted?* Technically, we all have the same 168 hours in a week. But over the course of that February, I realized something powerful. Sure, I wasted time like everyone else with internet scrolling and the like. But through multitasking—the much-maligned practice of doing multiple things at once—I had managed to create an extra forty-eight hours in my week.

"Bad" multitasking happens when we're trying to perform two incompatible tasks at once, like writing an email and participating in a conference call. You can't formulate cogent sentences while listening attentively to a separate conversation. But the multitasking I had intuitively adopted—what I'll dare to call "good" multitasking—enabled me to perform two *complementary* tasks at the same time, like exercising at the gym and listening to an audiobook, or calling my mother while preparing dinner, or taking in a theater performance with a business client. If I could legitimately do both tasks effectively, I counted them twice, so I'd mark down thirty minutes apiece for "call with Mom" and "cooking"—and ultimately ended up with 29% more time in my week than I'd expected.

In addition to optimizing my regular activities, I also looked for downtime that others would write off and tried to see what it was good for. A while back, I flew to St. Petersburg, Russia, and was battling jet lag the first day of my trip. I wandered around the city, exploring and trying desperately to soak in enough weak sunlight to reset my circadian rhythms. I was hungry, sleepy, and unfocused—not a great combination for any detail-oriented work. Even the thought of answering emails seemed overwhelming. But as I sat down for tea at a café, I was suddenly inspired, and cadged a pen and paper from the hostess. I had been reading on the plane: a compendium of essays by Peter Drucker, the great management theorist who had been a mentor to Marshall Goldsmith. The loose ideas that had been jangling around in my mind started to coalesce. Drucker was a master of strategic thinking, and inspired by my reading, I wrote these questions out:

- What should I spend my time doing?

- What are the 20% of my activities that will yield 80% of the results?

- What can I stop doing?

- How can I use constraints to my advantage?

- What are my hypotheses about the future—and how do they inform my actions today?

Over the next hour, I wrote pages of notes with answers to those questions, which set a useful strategic direction for me for the next year. (You might want to try it yourself.) Apparently, in the back of my sleep-addled brain, I'd been processing my Drucker reading and how it applied to my own life and business. As the Dutch researcher Ap Dijksterhuis has discovered, unconscious thought while we're distracted by other things can lead to better results than consciously weighing pros and cons—as happened during my St. Petersburg walkabout. As he notes, "unconscious processes have the capacity to work on different things in parallel and can integrate a large amount of information," and they seem to be better than conscious thought at "weighting the relative importance of different attributes."[1]

I hadn't realized that jet lag would be the optimal state for me to do my year's strategic planning. But as soon as I sensed it, I leaned in and took advantage of time that others would have marked as useless. Leverage enables us to get more out of less.

The other question we need to learn to ask ourselves is this: *How can I do something once and make it count ten times?* In a literal example, you can take one piece of content—let's say a blog post—and share it in different ways through social media. You can link to the blog itself on Facebook, post an excerpted quote on Twitter, upload a related image to Instagram, and share your key findings in a short piece on LinkedIn. With just a bit more effort, maybe 10% of the effort of writing the post in the first place, you've maximized its distribution potential and ensured that many more readers will discover it. And yet, we rarely do the same in other, even more significant, areas of our lives.

Let's take the example of Nihar Chhaya, a member of my Recognized Expert community and an executive coach to *Fortune* 500 companies. In November 2019, Nihar traveled to London to attend Thinkers50, a gathering of business authors and executives dubbed the "Oscars of management thinking" by the *Financial Times*. It's a pricey event, compounded by travel expenses, including airfare from Dallas, where Nihar lives. Attending also meant he'd be taking time away from his young daughter—so he had to make it count.

Most people would focus on the obvious: making sure they introduced themselves to a lot of people at the gathering, or angling to network with certain attendees. But Nihar took a far more holistic view of how to get value from attending.

After the event, he wrote about his experience for *Forbes*, where he was a regular contributor, realizing that doing so could help him meet his publishing obligations for the site. The article enabled him to give shout-outs to some of the luminaries he'd met there, including Amy Edmondson of Harvard Business School and Stew Friedman of the Wharton School of the University of Pennsylvania. Sharing the article on social media gave him another opportunity to solidify the new connections and ensure that they remembered who he was.

Writing the piece also had a few other benefits. It gave him a reason to reach out to one of the Thinkers50 cofounders for an interview, building a new relationship. It helped him codify his own learnings from the event, so it could serve as professional development. And given that Thinkers50 is a high-end event, it enhanced his credentials and social proof.

Most people do one thing and then stop, especially if that thing is time-consuming, onerous, or expensive. But when we can make one activity count more than once, we have a unique competitive advantage. So often, we feel powerless about our time and our schedule, which cripples our ability to think and act in our long-term interest. But we all have agency. The secret is upending the time limitations we all have so that we can think in new ways. We have to kill two—or more—birds with one stone. That means understanding what matters most to us, and then leveraging the resources at our disposal.

Leveraging for Your Relationships

For most of us, relationships are extraordinarily important. Yet we've all heard stories about the high-powered executive who can't seem to make time for his family, but professes that they're the reason behind everything he does. What would it look like if work and family weren't a zero-sum game, but instead represented a series of deliberate strategic choices?

Phil Van Nostrand is a photographer in New York City, earning thousands to shoot weddings or events. But for years, he accepted a $500-a-day assignment to cover a "random JavaScript tech conference in San Francisco." Why? He's originally from Santa Barbara, and the annual conference paid for his cross-country flight. "I could spend a week with my family, and it felt like a free trip home for a half day's work," he says.

I've done the same, accepting lower rates to speak at conferences in North Carolina—events I would have turned down anywhere else—because they gave me an opportunity to visit my mother, now in her eighties. I also looked for opportunities to bring her along on adventures, carting her to a January teaching gig in Kazakhstan (she was a hit with the students, who took us sightseeing in subzero temperatures) and to lecture tours of Vietnam, Singapore, and France. When we're clear about our true priorities, it's a lot easier to optimize accordingly.

Leveraging for the Life You Want

Another powerful way to frame your choices is to understand your ideal lifestyle. Where, and how, do you want to live? And what would it look like for you to stand up for that vision?

That's what Annmarie Neal, a successful executive, asked herself. Life would have been simpler if she'd been willing to move to a corporate hub—New York, or San Francisco, or maybe Dallas or Chicago. But for more than twenty-five years, she's instead lived in a small Colorado town, nearly ninety minutes away from Denver. "I fell in love with the 'work hard, play hard' values and lifestyle of the state," she says. "But the truth is that the mountains feed my soul." She wasn't willing to compromise, even when it meant turning down plum C-level jobs, such as the head of talent for a Zurich-based company.

But she's been surprisingly successful at making her case nonetheless, including to Cisco, where she served for five years as the chief talent officer, and in her current role of leading talent for a large private equity firm. "For an innovation economy worker, the best ideas may come from taking a long walk or two-mile swim," she says. "The desk is not the place where real work may happen. My line is, 'Do you want to hire the best person for the role, or the best person in your zip code?'" Many of us may not feel empowered to take such a bold stance, and Annmarie was certainly helped by her strong reputation and experience. But even for younger professionals, it's far more possible than they might imagine to leverage their lifestyle choices in small ways.

Phil, the photographer, routinely accepts unconventional payment terms that help him create the kind of "epic freelance life" that he wants. For example, he bartered with one client who specialized in the sale of luxury woolen goods. "It'd be a shoot for $500 plus a scarf," he says, "and these are $800 cashmere scarves from Mongolia—they're amazing." It's far more than he'd spend for a scarf on his own, but he loves having them. "I have a big throw on my couch, a basket of scarves in my room that I wear regularly in the winter, and I gifted my sister one as well."

Similarly, an acquaintance who owns a hip Mexican restaurant in Brooklyn needed new photos for his website. Phil's typical fee would have been $1,200, so the owner suggested $800 plus a $400 restaurant credit. "I was happy to do the exchange, and it cost them really nothing to do that bonus," Phil recalls.

He has also volunteered to shoot "glamour shots" of homeless cats for Koneko, a cat café in his neighborhood. "I came over one morning before the doors opened, and with their best cat person, we got the cats doing all these little poses. It was two hours, and I got hundreds of dollars [in store credit]. I was in that cat café for almost a year straight, just eating their food and hanging out with cats with friends."

Through his flexibility and creativity, Phil has created a lifestyle—replete with fashion and dining—that otherwise wouldn't have been available to him. But it's possible when you decide to leverage for the life you want.

Leveraging for Your Professional Goals

What if we didn't think about "work" and "life" as quite so separate? What if we could find ways to combine them that actually enhanced both?

That's what Christina Guthier wondered. She was a young German doctoral student who was planning a vacation to visit a friend in Canada. She and her husband had loved their first trip to New York City a few years prior, so they decided to add a week in the city to their visit. The trip was recreational, but Christina wondered if she could leverage it professionally as well. She asked her thesis advisor if he had any contacts in New York, and he did: a professor at the City College of New York, who invited Christina to speak as a guest lecturer. Impressed with her research, the professor ended up citing her in his next book.

In addition to harnessing the professional benefits of vacation time, Christina also looked for opportunities to do the reverse. She made friends with an Australian professor who urged her to come to the University of South Australia as a guest researcher, but the timing never seemed right. When she got pregnant, though, she realized there might be an opportunity. Once her daughter was nine months old, Christina, ready to return to work, boarded a plane with her husband, just in time for him to take two warm and sunny months of paternity leave while she collaborated with new colleagues.

Christina isn't the only professional who's found creative ways to blend travel and professional development. Phil the photographer has done that too. "What I had dreamed of, when I started taking pictures, was that someone would fly me somewhere. I wouldn't have to pay for anything, and I would get to travel for free. And that was it." He'd become friends with a woman who was an expert in historical fashion design. "Before she met me," Phil says, "she'd design a gown for Carnival in Venice, and then go with her friends. But taking pictures on your iPhone is not quite the same thing as having a real photographer follow you around." So one year, she invited Phil to join them, and he's now traveled with her twice to Venice, once to Paris and Versailles, and once to "the south of France during lavender season."

Not everyone would think it's such a great deal. "If you talk to any old-school photographers, [they'd say] I should be getting paid for my time in Venice," he says. But that's not how he sees it. His friend isn't wealthy, "so squeezing money out of [her and her friends], it wouldn't be satisfying for anybody," he says. "They wouldn't have a budget for me anyway. And to get a free vacation is priceless."

But it's not just the free vacation. Phil retains the rights to the photos from the trip, which are lush and atmospheric. "I could sell one of those prints," he says. "And I know that that's going to open doors to someone who sees it and thinks of me for a magazine shoot, which is one of my bigger goals." Ultimately, he says, "my philosophy is that value is not always just in dollar amounts. I'm just looking at the long-term value." Of course, he's glad to take on high-paying corporate work, and that's necessary to pay his rent and expenses. But snapshots of executives at a podium don't necessarily demonstrate his unique artistic vision. "Usually you're either getting money or fame, but you're rarely getting both," he says.

Too many of us get waylaid by easy money or other people's expectations of what success looks like. You can't become a preeminent photographer—the kind who shoots magazine covers or has billboards in Times Square—by doing what's easy. You have to be willing to wait, to build relationships, and to make strategic trade-offs that may seem ridiculous to others today but could prove critical in the future. When you do, you're able to make choices that, in the long run, set you up for far more success.

Leveraging the Currency We Have

We've talked about the reasons behind the choices you make—leveraging to benefit your relationships, or your lifestyle, or your professional goals. But now let's talk about the mechanics of how we do it.

The obvious thing to leverage is money. You can use it to buy something you want; for instance, you could pay a house cleaner so you have more time with your family. Or you can accept less of it, or forgo it, in order to build your connections or experience (as Phil has done with his photography).

But what's less often appreciated is that money isn't the only form of currency. Years ago, I dated a successful artist. Her paintings sold for a good amount of money, but after the gallery's 50% cut, she certainly wasn't rich. The true currency she had acquired was reputation. She was represented by a well-known gallery and had been reviewed in all the right publications. And that meant collectors—typically financiers with huge incomes—were keen to meet her.

I'd tag along to dinners at New York City hot spots, gala fundraisers, and even a trip to an Aspen vacation home. These were extraordinarily successful businesspeople; at most parties, they would be swarmed by admirers. If money were the only salient metric, my then-girlfriend would have been of little interest. But for people who care about art, the excitement of spending time with a prominent artist was the ultimate currency. And, of course, it was a win-win: an opportunity for us to enjoy events we wouldn't have had access to, and for her to meet other artists and collectors.

Clearly, not all of us are professional artists (or major league athletes or rock stars). But with planning and forethought, most professionals can develop their own forms of currency. Through writing my book *Stand Out* and developing my Recognized Expert course, I came to realize there are three key components to becoming a recognized expert in your company or field. They are:

Content creation. You can't become known for your ideas if other people don't know what they are. Thus, you need to find a way to create content, whether that's through writing articles, giving speeches, starting a podcast, making videos, holding lunch-and-learns, or whatever channel you prefer.

Social proof. People are busy, so you need to give them a reason to pay attention to what you say. Social proof—your demonstrated credibility—is a quick way to do that. It's especially powerful if you can find a way to connect yourself to brands and people they already know and trust. For instance, if you've written for or have been quoted in publications people have heard of, if you've consulted for or work for brand-name companies, if you're the head of a local professional association or an alumni group—those are all reasonable ways to demonstrate to others, at a glance, that you're worth listening to.

Network. Finally, creating content and being credible is essential, but if no one knows who you are, it still won't do you any good. You need to develop a network that can help you amplify your voice and spread the word about what you're doing (not to mention help you identify which ideas are good, and which aren't, in the first place).

Many professionals, especially if they're relatively senior, have developed one or even two of these pillars. And if they've been working to get their ideas heard and build an expert reputation, they might be frustrated that they're hitting a wall. The reason is that you need all three components. This is a situation where doubling down on the pillar you like the best simply doesn't help. You can write one hundred articles a month, but if they're all on your own blog and no one knows who you are, it still won't land you a book deal or a consulting contract.

Instead, the right move is to take the area where you're strong—the currency you have—and strategically leverage it to gain the currency you lack. For instance:

- If you're good at creating content but don't have social proof, you can show samples of your work and pitch yourself to write for a high-profile publication.

- If you're good at creating content but don't have a network, you can ask to interview someone, and thereby build a relationship.

- If you have strong social proof but aren't good at creating content, you could get someone else to write about you or quote you.

- If you have strong social proof but no network, you can invite someone to speak to an organization where you're on the board.

- If you have a strong network but haven't created content, you could start a podcast and interview your many friends.

- If you have a strong network but no social proof, you can tap your friends to invite you to speak at universities where they teach or organizations they lead.

Many people get frustrated because they're fixated on one form of currency, and if they don't have it, they curse their luck. ("I don't have enough money to do X" or "I didn't go to an Ivy League school, so I can't do Y.") But there's almost never just one way to do something.

Get creative about leveraging the forms you have, or can acquire, and trade that for other ones you want. It's those strategic trade-offs that enable us to make better and smarter choices about the long term. If you're interested in learning where you stand on each of these three pillars, I've created a Recognized Expert self-assessment, which you can download for free at https://dorieclark.com/toolkit.

It should be clear by now that optimizing for the present, or the short term, will almost never get us to where we want to be in the end. And it's also true that we rarely have exactly what we need for long-term success. That's why we make strategic trade-offs. Because when we leverage the assets we have to get those we want, we're able to reach what otherwise would have seemed impossible.

Reaching our goals can be a slow process. We need guidance and support to get there. But what if we don't currently have trusted advisers around us? Or we'd like to find more of them? That's what comes next.

Remember:

Ask yourself some of my favorite questions for achieving leverage:

- What should I spend my time doing?

- What are the 20% of my activities that will yield 80% of the results?

- What can I stop doing?

- How can I use constraints to my advantage?

- What are my hypotheses about the future, and how do they inform my actions today?

- How can I do something once and make it count ten times?

- Where, and how, do I want to live? What would it look like to stand up for that vision?

- What are the ways I could combine work and my personal life to make both more enjoyable?

- What forms of currency (e.g., connections, writing for high-profile publications, hosting a podcast, memberships in certain clubs, etc.) do I have that I could leverage to obtain different forms of currency?

7

The Right People, the Right Rooms

When I moved to New York City a few years back, I soon came to a stunning realization: I didn't have any friends. I had professional acquaintances, of course, and I could scare up a networking meeting if I wanted to. Lunch on Thursday? Coffee on Monday afternoon? Filling business hours was no problem. But once I'd finished with the hubbub of unpacking and I got back into normal rhythms, I discovered that every evening on my calendar was free—into infinity.

I had to do something. I'd told people I was moving to the city, but they still thought of me as living in Boston. When there was a party or a dinner, I wasn't top of mind. And the people I did know were casual acquaintances, not necessarily friends who might invite me to hang out on a Friday or Saturday night. Staring out at the glittering lights of the skyline, the city humming below me, I wondered: How could I find a way to connect with interesting people and build the circle I desperately wanted?

I knew one thing: I didn't want to be a victim. I didn't want to complain that no one was reaching out, or that things were unfair, or that it was "just too hard" to make friends in New York. There had to be something proactive that I could do—something within my control. I flashed back to my mother's advice from childhood, deployed whenever I wasn't invited to a birthday party or class-mates had planned an adventure without me: "To *get* an invita-tion, you have to *give* an invitation." It's still good advice.

Too often, professionals—even smart, accomplished ones who have no problem pitching major clients or delivering on high-stakes engagements—assume they have no agency when it comes to networking. They think, "Why would he want to meet with me?" or "She's way too busy" or "I wouldn't want to impose" or "I don't want to look needy." And it's true: not everyone wants to have coffee with you. I can guarantee that Jeff Bezos is probably too busy, and Warren Buffett would turn you (or me) down. But that doesn't mean *no one* wants to connect. In fact, what I realized during that lonely New York summer was that other people are often just as hungry to connect. They're waiting for an invitation that never comes—and if you're the one to step up and proffer it, they'll be enormously grateful.

I found a Mexican restaurant I liked, with decent acoustics and circular tables that could seat ten, and set about my invitations. I started with people I knew, but quickly broadened it: I'd some-times recruit a cohost, and we'd each be responsible for inviting four guests so we could cross-pollinate our networks.

The format was simple: the first half hour was informal, to allow people time to arrive and order. Next, we'd go around the table to do introductions, break for a few moments when dinner arrived to allow the server to distribute the meals, and then go around the table once more with a more introspective question everyone could answer, such as "What are you proudest of this year?" or "What are you looking forward to in the fall?" or "What's the most surprising lesson you've learned in the past few years?"

I've now hosted more than sixty dinners with hundreds of attendees and over time have built a reputation as a connector in a city where I hardly knew anyone. During Covid-19, I shifted the format to virtual and began hosting them over Zoom with my friend Alisa Cohn (the executive coach/freestyle rapper from chapter 3), which enabled us to preserve the general format but with the added opportunity to invite guests from around the world.

Not everyone you invite will become your best friend. The truth is, many of the guests never followed up or said thank you. Some canceled at the last minute or even ghosted altogether. But some have become valued business connections. I began a collaboration with *Newsweek*, hosting a weekly video interview series, as a result of meeting an editor at a dinner gathering.

Other attendees have become close friends, people I really can invite over on a Friday or Saturday night. And, in line with one of my primary goals for the dinners, I'm not the only one who's benefited. "I think about you every time I catch up with Evan," one attendee wrote me. "He was instrumental in helping me raise my first round of capital [for my startup] and is now an adviser. I wouldn't have known him were it not for you inviting me to one of your dinners."

If Networking's So Great,
Why Don't We Do More of It?

The benefits of networking are clear: you can meet interesting people, learn new things, discover trends, and—just maybe—land a new job or client or board seat that can transform your career. And yet many of us resist it, or endlessly put it off to another day.

Partly that's because it seems like a lot of work. Sure, you can ask someone to coffee, but turning that into a real relationship? It's an investment, and one that many adults haven't consciously made since college, when potential friends lived next door in the dorm. As adult professionals, with job responsibilities and perhaps families to tend to, it's trickier.

And it's true that turning someone into a genuine friend takes a serious investment of time. Research by professor Jeffrey Hall at the University of Kansas shows that it takes about fifty hours of exposure to move someone from acquaintance to casual friend, another ninety hours to move them up to actual friend status, and more than two hundred hours to turn someone into a close friend.[1] Who has time like that these days?

But even the relationships you form with casual acquaintances can be transformative (a principle discussed in the sociologist Mark Granovetter's seminal 1973 paper "The Strength of Weak Ties"[2]). I met a woman back in 2015 when she was invited to a dinner by my cohosts. Since then, I've invited her to a couple additional dinners, and she's hosted me on her podcast and interviewed me for her book—a pleasant but light connection. Meanwhile, she referred me to a business opportunity that has brought in more than $1.1 million over the past five years. You just never know.

But there's another reason—even more salient than time—that stops many professionals from the relationship building that is so important for their careers: networking makes them feel dirty.

A study by Francesca Gino of Harvard Business School and her colleagues showed that many professionals felt ashamed and inauthentic when it came to networking.[3] But it's not just anxiety in the moment. Even *contemplating* networking can trigger "dirty" feelings. Gino and her colleagues had participants rate the desirability of various consumer products, from cleaning supplies like soaps and toothpastes to "neutral" items like Post-it notes. For participants who first read a story about professional networking, the cleaning products suddenly became far more compelling.

Of course, not everyone is triggered by networking in this way. But among the people who are, Gino and her colleagues discovered two important caveats that provide a path forward for those who just can't bring themselves to network. First, transactional networking, in which you're hoping to obtain a specific benefit ("I want to meet that venture capitalist so she can invest in my company"), feels much grimier than simply networking to make friends. And second, junior-level professionals often feel more conflicted about networking than senior professionals do. There are two possible explanations here. One is that the senior professionals rose through the ranks *because* they enjoyed, or at least didn't mind, networking. The other is that the senior professionals don't feel as stressed because they have the status and connections to help ensure the relationships they forge will be reciprocal (you might introduce me to a potential client, but I might be able to do the same for you).

Gino's insights here are crucial: what stresses people out isn't networking per se; it's the idea of using people. In actuality, there are three types of networking: short term, long term, and infinite horizon. It's short-term, transactional networking that gives the whole enterprise a bad name, and I'm going to suggest we avoid it whenever humanly possible. True networking isn't about trying to get something as fast as you can. That's a caricature of *bad* networking, yet people hold it up as an excuse for not engaging.

When we network for the long term or with an infinite horizon—that is, when we set out to make friends and build relationships, rather than simply get something—it feels entirely different. Like the junior people in Gino's study, we need to take the time to understand how we can help others, so we're not simply takers in this equation. It may seem complicated ("What would I ever have to offer him that he doesn't already have?"), but there are strategies and ways to discover the hidden value you can bring.

So let's talk about how to do this right.

Short-Term Networking

"So, there is a guy who reached out earlier this week and asked to do a Zoom call with me," one of my coaching clients told me. They're in a professional group together, so my client said yes. And then the sneak attack. "He's a nice guy," my client said, "but in just the first ten minutes of us going over our backgrounds, he asked me [for a big favor]. I was taken aback. I would never ask a stranger for something like that, even if we just happen to be in the same group. I don't want to be a jerk, so I usually say I'll help, but I feel pretty used afterward."

We've all been there: the innocent meetup that turns into an ambush. My client certainly isn't the only one. The next week, another friend reached out for my advice. He'd been getting to know a colleague over the past couple of months—a slower burn—and they'd had four video chats together. And then the new colleague made a significant ask, one that required a great deal of political capital. "It made me wonder," my friend said, "was this his plan all along? Had he been pacing it out, pretending to be interested in getting to know me, and just waiting to make his ask?"

I can't count the number of times a literal or virtual stranger has asked me for a personal introduction to magazine editors or celebrity colleagues. Sometimes, in the short term, aggressive maneuvers work: people fold and say yes in the moment. But in the long run, it never does. Because when people feel used, they're never willing to help again.

We can't avoid short-term networking completely. There are times when it's necessary—maybe you've been laid off and desperately need a job. But desperation is never attractive, and you should never try to forge new relationships under those circumstances. Some professionals wildly misinterpret the adage that "it can't hurt to ask." Certainly, it's important to ask for things we feel we deserve, like a raise, and if you're polite with certain requests, like a hotel upgrade, you might get lucky. But that doesn't mean you have carte blanche to ask anyone for anything.

In true moments of need, it's perfectly appropriate to turn to your friends. They know you, your character, and your abilities, and they're willing to expend their social capital on your behalf. They might be willing to connect you with strangers who can assist—for instance, if there's a job opening at their company. But the connection request is viewed differently because it's coming from your mutual friend, whom the other person already knows and trusts. If you're reaching out cold when you're in "I need" mode, you're unlikely to get very far—and per Francesca Gino's research, you'll probably feel dirty while doing it.

The strategy I follow personally, and recommend to others, is *no asks for a year.* I learned it the hard way. Once I met a woman who was a bit of a rising star, a journalist with a well-received new book. She'd spoken at a major conference where I hoped to be invited. We'd enjoyed a group dinner together and traded a couple of emails back and forth when I decided to inquire. I took pains to be subtle: "Congratulations on your recent talk!" I wrote. "I loved the video. One of my goals is to speak there one day. Do you happen to have any advice about how one might break in?"

As far as things go, this wasn't a bad email. Unlike my friend's "favor assailant," I certainly wasn't asking her directly for an introduction or a nomination: I was only seeking general information. But in retrospect, I realized even that was too much, too soon. She had a high-enough profile that she was probably deluged with connection requests. Even though I felt worthy to be her peer, it was easy to see how all the entreaties from people she barely knew would begin to sound the same.

I could imagine how the script played out in her head: she would reply with helpful general advice, only to receive a perky follow-up note that said something like, "Thanks so much, that's really helpful! By the way, would you mind introducing me to [person in charge]? Based on what you said, I think I'd be a perfect fit as a speaker." To avoid having to say no—implicitly or explicitly—and risk her own political capital, she didn't let the conversation get to that point. She knew, or at least thought she knew, what was coming.

I never heard back. I was stung by the realization that she probably viewed me as no different from the people who only wanted to be her friend because she could introduce them to her editor or get them on a particular stage. I vowed that I would never let anyone even get close to that assumption again. Therefore: no asks for a year.

Of course, that doesn't mean you don't invite people to events (the point of friendship is to get to know each other better) or ask minor questions where they can assist (say, what's the name of the transcription service they use?). What I'm talking about is asks that require political capital, which very successful people fend off from others all the time. You never want to put yourself into that category. Waiting a year to ask for any favors prevents anyone from inferring that you have an agenda. And frankly, it stops you from having one, even subconsciously. It lets you step back and concentrate on building a genuine friendship.

Long-Term Relationship Building

A far better alternative to "I need something, so what can you give me?" is to focus on long-term networking. You don't have a specific ask in mind: all you know is that this person, or this group, is worth getting to know.

That's how I felt more than a decade ago when I started writing for *Harvard Business Review*. The authors who wrote for it were professors, consultants, and corporate leaders at the top of their game. I didn't have any specific networking goals in mind, but I knew that good things would happen if I put myself in the right room. So I created a spreadsheet of the institutional affiliations of HBR contributors, determining which ones lived in Boston (where I resided at the time). Then I invited them for coffee, always offering to come to a convenient location of their choice.

The moment you identify a commonality with someone you'd like to meet, or a group you'd like to get more involved in, you can leverage that shared experience to connect more deeply. People are usually wary of lower-level aspirants who seem to be approaching them because they want something. But when you can approach someone as a peer ("I'm a fellow contributor to HBR" or "I'm also a member of XYZ group"), they're often eager to connect and trade notes. I call this the *press your advantage* strategy.

I tried to add value where I could: if the contributors I met had a book coming out, I'd offer to interview them about it in another publication. Taking the initiative to reach out and be helpful in promoting their work positioned me as a valued colleague, and enabled me to break into the network quickly—all of which made it easier for me to connect with each subsequent contributor. Those early connections led to coauthoring opportunities, as well as an introduction to a top-ranked business school in France, where I taught for several years.

But what if there isn't a group of peers or colleagues that you'd like to break into? What if no such thing exists? In that case, you can create one yourself.

"I had zero network, no contacts, no job, and no friends here," Tanvi Gautam recalls. That's what her life looked like in 2011, when she moved to Singapore from the US. Tanvi had joined Twitter around the same time and thought it might be a way to make connections—but the online conversation seemed to be very North America–centric. She'd have to roll up her sleeves to build a community. "I crowdsourced and curated a list of fifty women from Asia to follow [on Twitter] that got a tremendous audience," she recalls. "I then started noticing all these tweetchats, but none was happening in Asia. So I launched one for HR professionals, and it became one of the first internationally trending Twitter chats to come out of Asia."

She didn't know exactly what the online community she built would lead to, but she knew these were the people she wanted to connect with. "We had CHROs, CEOs, authors, thought leaders, and more, all joining from all over the world," she recalls. As a result of running the group, Tanvi, now a professor at Singapore Management University, has received prestigious speaking invitations, been featured in newspapers and magazines, and was lauded by the Society for Human Resource Management as a social media influencer for six years in a row.

Besides starting your own group, another possibility is to identify people, or groups of people, you'd like to get to know based on your long-term future goals. If you think you might like to move to Los Angeles in the next few years, you could deliberately start getting to know Californians, so you can determine what it's really like to live there and have a network of friends in place when you move. Similarly, if you're interested in doing adjunct teaching down the line, it's not a bad idea to develop new contacts in academia who might advise you.

The point is to build connections with high-quality people. That's what Jenny Fernandez did. Early in her career at a consumer packaged goods company, she built a strong relationship with her manager, who was promoted to become chief marketing officer for the China office. "With the distance and twelve-to-thirteen-hour time difference, it was challenging to keep in touch" in those pre–social media days, Jenny recalls. "But I always reached out, let her know how I was doing and about my career progress, and what was happening in the division."

It would have been easy to lose touch over time. But Jenny's commitment to staying connected paid off. "Four years later, she requested me to join her in China as she embarked in a new role as

Asia Pacific region CMO." She tapped Jenny to lead business strategy and marketing for a major product line in thirteen countries.

Too many professionals take an "out of sight, out of mind" approach to their networks. But playing the long game means staying focused on, and connected to, the great people you meet along the way. Some professionals, seeing an opportunity before them, pounce prematurely—the equivalent of asking for a favor ten minutes into an introductory phone call. But often you can get a more meaningful result, for both of you, by being patient and putting the other person's interests first.

Marketing consultant Kris Marsh saw that principle come to life in her relationship with her longtime car dealer. "We had lunch to catch up one day," she recalls, "and he mentioned the dealership was trying to connect with the next generation. I could have tried to sell him a contract." But she didn't. At the time, she was teaching an advertising class at Central Michigan University and suggested that her students could work with him to devise a campaign for his dealership. "It was a win-win," she says. "My students got great experience and he got a great advertising campaign, which he implemented."

The most powerful client relationships don't come from you pushing an agenda or shoving a sales pitch down someone's throat. They come from developing so much trust that the other person asks if you'll consider working with them. Through their work together on the student project, the dealer got to know Kris on a far deeper level: he'd seen her in action. "He mentioned that he was so impressed with the leadership I demonstrated in my classroom that he wondered what I could do to develop his leadership team," she says. "I've led several leadership development workshops for his team now, and he's referred me to several other clients."

It's certainly possible that the car dealer could have accepted the free help from Kris's class and then vanished. Perhaps her generosity might have cost her a contract. But someone only focused on cadging free help probably wouldn't have been the best client, anyway. As Adam Grant, professor at the Wharton School at the University of Pennsylvania, wrote in his acclaimed book *Give and Take*, you don't want to be a sucker—don't keep giving to people who never reciprocate. But if you begin your interactions from a place of generosity, the right people will notice and will be inspired to help you, too. As Kris says, "It's business built on trust and a genuine interest to help each other."

Long-term networking isn't about getting a job next week or next year. Instead, it's about cultivating connections with people you admire and want to spend more time with. We don't know precisely what form it will take. But when you're in the right rooms with the right people, it creates the conditions for opportunity.

Infinite Horizon Networking

Perhaps the most gratifying form of networking is what I call infinite horizon networking. It's pure, no-agenda relationship building. Because when you have zero goals or expectations—only a fundamental interest in who the person is—you can enjoy the experience and let it unfold organically.

Quite logically, we optimize our networks based on who we are now, or what we imagine our future plans to be. But of course, we can't predict the future. We spend years developing relationships in our industry—only to decide we want to switch fields. Or we cultivate deep community ties—only to move across the country because of a too-good-to-refuse job offer.

The answer is to embrace infinite horizon networking. The person you meet may have no professional relevance to you whatsoever: you're a journalist and they're an astronaut, or you're an accountant and they're a politician. But given enough time, career and life trajectories change, and you may veer much closer to each other. Even more profoundly, you can influence each other in unexpected ways—sparking a line of inquiry, awakening an old passion, or inspiring a creative solution. Your life looks different, and better, because of their presence.

That's how it happened for Hayim Makabee, the founder of an influencer marketing startup called KashKlik. Born in Rio de Janeiro, Hayim immigrated to Israel nearly thirty years ago. Wanting to give back, he started volunteering for an immigrant aid organization. In the process, he befriended a staffer named Ricardo, and together they helped organize a number of meetups, lectures, and holiday celebrations.

Ricardo later took a job at a startup accelerator based at the Technion, Israel's prestigious technical university—and he didn't forget his connection to Hayim. "Ricardo invited me to pitch my startup to potential investors in an event organized by [the accelerator]," Hayim recalls. "Later, Ricardo also was responsible for receiving delegations of Brazilian entrepreneurs that came to visit the Technion. Several times, he invited me to present to these foreign delegations and tell them about my personal experience in the Israeli startup ecosystem."

The benefit was substantial. "One of the entrepreneurs I met in these delegations later invited me to join the board of his startup company," Hayim says. "Today I'm an executive board member and have equity in this Brazilian startup." When he started volunteering for the immigrant aid nonprofit, Hayim never could have predicted that it would lead to him joining a company's board of directors. He didn't know he'd befriend Ricardo, much less that Ricardo would ever be in a position to help him professionally. But when you have no agenda whatsoever in your networking, except to meet interesting people, help others, and learn new things, anything can happen.

Making It Big

That's what Laura Gassner Otting realized as she took it all in: her name in lights, emanating from *Good Morning America*'s Times Square studio, with a pumped-up audience cheering her on. With more than a million books published every single year, it's almost impossible for a new author to get noticed. Laura's first book, *Limitless*, wasn't published by a major New York house, and she wasn't a celebrity or a reality TV star. She was a mom and entrepreneur from suburban Boston whose book had only been out for a month when she got the invitation of a lifetime.

How did she pull it off? It starts with an infinite horizon.

So often, people want the "magic bullet" that will get them the speaking gig or the contract or the on-air appearance. But the magic bullet isn't one thing. It's everything.

For Laura, it started with her resource guide. For fifteen years, she'd run her own recruiting firm. Eventually she sold it to her employees, and after a TEDx talk she gave sparked some inquiries about speaking professionally, she started thinking about it. But where do you start? What do you charge?

To learn, she joined a Facebook group of professional speakers. "When I was first invited into that group," she recalls, "I was so intimidated by all the people that were there. These are incredible people who are making $30,000 or $40,000 or $50,000 a talk, and I was like, 'Well, I don't belong here at all, and they're going to figure that out pretty quickly.'" But instead of hiding in the background and keeping quiet, she had a different strategy: "I'm going to take and I'm going to learn, but every time I take and I learn, I'm going to also add that resource back in."

Her first question was how to structure a speaking contract. The group had created a database where members could upload their contracts for others to view, but it was chaotic and disorganized—a huge amount of work to sift through. Laura decided to tackle the challenge. "I just went through them and I made notes to myself," she says. "Like, this is what most people do about travel. This is what most people do about filming. This is what most people do about intellectual property. And then I shared it to the group."

She created a clear, easily digestible guide that collected best practices and made the amorphous data useful to everyone. Before long, she says, "I became part of the cool kids in this group, because I kept giving back. I learned something about book publishing, I learned something about podcasts, and I would just share the resources over and over again. And all of us can do that." Through her willingness to be helpful, she says, "I started creating these online friendships with people that I never met before, who I'd be totally scared to actually call in real life."

One of them was Mitch Joel, a prominent Canadian author and digital marketing expert. One day, he posted in the group that he'd be in Boston for a conference—would anyone like to meet for lunch? Laura raised her hand, and an in-person friendship was born. But that's only the beginning. Mitch and Laura kept in touch, and several months later, he sent her an unusual text message. As Laura recalls, "He's like, 'Hey, my company is actually sponsoring an event tomorrow and Joe Biden [then the former vice president] is the keynote speaker. And I know that you have a background in politics. What are you doing tomorrow?'"

To be clear, this was a thoughtful invitation, but not a convenient one. Laura lives in Boston, and Mitch's event was in Montreal. She'd have to buy a plane ticket and change all her plans for the very next day. "I could have easily said, 'No, no, no, I don't want to do that. I shouldn't spend the money. It seems like a boondoggle,'" Laura recalls. But she didn't. She rescheduled her meetings and spent the day at the event with Mitch, including a meet-and-greet with Biden.

When you engage in infinite horizon networking, you never know what's ultimately going to come of it. "If you do good things with good people, good stuff always seems to come," Laura says. It turns out, one good thing was Mitch whispering in the ear of the conference organizer, Scott: "Hey, Laura has a book coming out in two months, and you should have her as one of your speakers." Scott had a series of leadership conferences coming up—massive ones, with thousands of attendees and speakers like human rights advocate Malala Yousafzai. Laura understood her place in the pecking order: she wouldn't get paid for speaking. "When you're first starting out, that happens a lot," she says. Scott was willing to bulk order her book, though, so she embarked on a speaking tour of Canada.

On the last stop, one of the speakers was Robin Roberts, a host of *Good Morning America* and a hero of Laura's. Laura desperately wanted to meet her, but didn't see how she could. She told the event's emcee, whom she'd befriended over the course of the tour, about her disappointment. "So he literally takes my book from the pile and hands it to me. And he's like, 'Here, sign it, make it really good. And I'll make sure she gets it.'" Laura did her part, writing a heartfelt message about how and why Robin inspired her. And the emcee did his, literally chasing Robin out to her car as she departed and putting Laura's book in her hands. Robin read the book on her flight home, tweeted about it to her million-plus Twitter followers, and told her producer, "Book her."

"Did I know, when I was helping put those contract notes together, that that would lead to my friendship with Mitch, which would lead to meeting Scott, which would lead to being on stage, which would lead to Robin Roberts, which would lead to this emcee helping me to get in front of her?" Laura asks. "No. But if you go into life with the idea that you're serving others, that's going to keep coming back to you in multitudes."

When you connect to others with an infinite horizon—no agenda whatsoever other than being helpful and deepening your relationships with interesting people—that's how opportunity happens. It's also how I found myself onstage at the Grammys.

That Time I Helped Produce a Grammy-Winning Jazz Album

It was February 2017, and I was out of breath. I'd just sprinted to the front of the auditorium in my tuxedo; I had mere moments to reach the stage and help accept the Grammy Award for Best Large Jazz Ensemble Album. After all, they have to keep the show moving. I blinked through the klieg lights into the vast, darkened auditorium and smiled before they hustled us backstage for photos.

How on earth did I get there? After all, I wasn't a jazz musician, or even a jazz connoisseur; I can't tell Miles Davis from Dizzy Gillespie from Thelonious Monk. What led me to become an assistant producer on that jazz album was my skill in another arena: networking.

I'll break down the process so you can get a sense of how it worked:

1. When I first moved to New York City, I followed my outreach strategy and researched other *Harvard Business Review* authors in the area. I ended up having coffee with Daniel Gulati, a venture capitalist who lived in the city at the time. A few days later, Daniel was scheduled to speak on a panel at the New School for Social Research. Apparently they needed an extra speaker, and Daniel asked if I'd like to join.

2. In the audience was Michael Roderick, a consultant and former Broadway producer who came up to me afterward and wanted to connect. We eventually decided to cohost networking dinners together.

3. Several months later, Michael invited Selena Soo to one of them—an entrepreneur I went on to profile in my book *Entrepreneurial You.*

4. A few months after that, a psychologist and executive coach named Ben Michaelis asked Selena to help him invite folks to a networking breakfast he was organizing, and she asked me to join.

5. At the breakfast, finally, that's where I met Kabir Sehgal. Kabir was a bit of a Renaissance man: a *New York Times*–bestselling author who also worked in finance and was a naval intelligence officer. His books ranged from a collection of poetry coauthored with Deepak Chopra to a study of the civil rights movement to a chronicle of the history of money. In short, a guy who knows how to optimize for interesting.

It turns out Kabir was a serious jazz musician and had produced a number of records. His next passion project, I learned, was writing the libretto for an opera. I immediately realized I could help him make some connections. This was before I joined the BMI Workshop, so I didn't have a special "in" in the music world. But because I'd developed a variety of infinite horizon connections, I knew plenty of musicians, including opera singers and opera composers. Inspired by wanting to help Kabir, I decided to throw a party so they could all get to know one another. So one July evening, I invited more than a dozen musicians I knew to my rooftop.

At the event, Kabir connected with a collaborator, and they began working on an opera together. Months later, Kabir, who wanted to repay the favor, was working on another project and sent me this note: "Dorie, is it OK if I sneak you in as an assistant producer of an album I'm releasing this summer, *Presidential Suite* by Ted Nash?" He said he thought it had a good chance at the Grammys, and he wasn't wrong. A few months later, the nominees were announced, and the Ted Nash Big Band was nominated for two. We won both.

I never thought I'd even attend the Grammys, much less walk the red carpet or help accept an award onstage. But open-ended networking, and reciprocal generosity, can allow incredible things to happen. So often, people get impatient about the networking process. They fume that it isn't working when one coffee or two meetups doesn't yield a new job or six-figure client. But my connection to Kabir—winding through connections from Daniel to Michael to Selena to Ben—is the rule rather than the exception.

The benefits of relationship building are far more powerful than we can imagine—largely *because* we can't fathom the exponential chain of connections and collisions they unleash. You can't predict what might arise from a given connection, which ones will bear fruit and which will go nowhere. That's impossibly frustrating if we're expecting a one-to-one correlation between input (a coffee date) and output (a new job offer). But when we're playing the long game, there's no rush: it's all part of the process of getting to know fascinating people.

Bringing Value to the Exchange

Francesca Gino (the Harvard Business School professor) and her colleagues realized that when you're unsure what you have to offer others, or suspect the answer is nothing, networking is a lot less pleasant. But if we look hard enough, everyone has something to offer. We may just have to get creative about it. It's great when you can directly meet a need someone has: they need an employee and your friend has the right background, or they need a recommendation for an IP attorney and you know a great one. But perfect fits like that are rare. We need to learn to traffic in other types of currency.

One is, quite simply, friendship and shared experiences. When Hayim Makabee worked with Ricardo in Israel, he had no way of knowing Ricardo would one day be in a position to help him. He wasn't "cultivating" him to help his company. But their time together on charitable projects built a strong bond. Similarly, Jenny Fernandez earned the respect of her former manager when they worked together, and she made a point of keeping up and checking in for years afterward, even though they were on opposite sides of the world. Peers love connecting with one another and trading notes on experiences. If you're part of a group, whether it's alumni of a particular school, contributors to a certain publication, or members of a given professional association, you can leverage that to reach out and forge connections.

You can also, where possible, contribute "sweat equity"—following the example of Heather Rothenberg, whom I profiled in my book *Reinventing You*. As a young graduate student, Heather built relationships with a slew of powerful leaders in her industry by volunteering to serve as the secretary of a professional group. It wasn't glamorous: she took notes and set up conference calls. But she built deep and trusting relationships with key leaders who later fought to hire her.

Additionally, senior leaders often get caught up in an "echo chamber." They want to hear different perspectives, but frequently don't—so if you're a frontline employee, or have a unique perspective based on the region where you work or the skills you've developed, your point of view may be very well received.

Another way to offer value is to help others make connections that will be interesting and valuable for them. The dinners I hosted in New York City enabled me to connect with attendees and catch up, but they also enabled other people to connect as well. My friend landing her startup adviser, or Kabir connecting with a panoply of opera professionals, never would have happened otherwise.

There's something sexy about the idea of becoming a "connector." It implies you're popular—the kind of person who knows everyone and can make things happen. Perhaps because of that, and its lingering Malcolm Gladwell glow,[4] many people pride themselves on being a connector without necessarily understanding the implicit rules. The first is that the connection should be consensual—meaning you've asked both parties if they'd like to meet. Way too often, I get emails like this one:

> By way of this email, I wanted to introduce you to [person], who is [bio]. He is already a fan of yours and your writing. Knowing how busy you are, I thought I would connect the two of you—to sync your superpowers of networking and connection.

On one hand, it's a lovely gesture—very complimentary, and clearly bringing together two people the introducer likes and respects. But flaws quickly emerge. If the author *really* knew how busy I was, he might have asked if I actually had time to meet his friend. And he seems to believe that "syncing our superpowers" is sufficient reason to connect, without explaining if there's a specific reason I'd want to meet the person.

In fact, of course, there is none. I hadn't expressed a desire to meet more people in X industry or with Y background. He and I had never discussed networking, or my openness to new connections, at all. Without that clarity, the connection he's made very quickly becomes a form of homework. Though it's not at all what he intended, he's assigned me the thirty-minute task of having a conversation with his friend so I can attempt to understand what we have in common and why it might be beneficial to develop a relationship.

The introducer made a common mistake, which is to assume that everyone is open to introductions and shares the same set of criteria for potential connections. Unless we know for sure—because the person has directly told us, or they're our best friend and we know everything about them—we have to ask.

Finally, you can break through and get noticed simply by being thoughtful and doing something different. The default networking request is "let's have coffee" or "let's have a video chat." There's nothing distinctive about that, so you risk blending in with all the other aspirants. Instead, think about what the other person might uniquely want or need. For instance, several weeks before I was scheduled to speak in Denmark, I received an email out of the blue from a woman named Sigrun Baldursdottir. "Copenhagen is known for being a city full of great clothing and interior design and decorations," she wrote. "I am a fashion designer with a master's degree in marketing and international business, and I have over fourteen years' experience working as a stylist."

She offered to take me on a shopping tour of Copenhagen at no charge, noting that "I have been watching your videos on your website, and I like your clothing style and I am very quick to find clothes you might like." If I were speaking in the United States, the offer wouldn't have been quite as enticing ("I can show you the best malls in Dallas!"). But she correctly surmised that the opportunity to tour the city with a local and shop for gifts (the holidays were approaching) was compelling. We ended up spending more than half a day together, and we're still in touch. By identifying areas where your skills overlap with the other person's needs, you can develop more-meaningful connections.

We all know that relationships with other people are crucial to our professional success, and to the quality of our lives. Yet many of us—catastrophizing about how networking will force us to become inauthentic users—neglect to develop the kind of genuine, transformative connections that any of us would want. Networking done right isn't about what it can get you today or tomorrow. It's about what kind of life you want to live and surrounding yourself with the kind of people you want coming along on that journey. Because when you're playing the long game, there are times it can feel incredibly hard or frustrating. How can we persevere nonetheless?

That's what we turn to next.

Remember:

- There are three types of networking:

  - **Short-term networking**, when you need something fast, like a job or a client. This is the type most likely to fall into the trap of using people, so do it sparingly and only with people you already have close relationships with.

  - **Long-term networking**, where you develop relationships with interesting people whom you admire and enjoy. These people may be potentially helpful to you in the future, but in indeterminate ways.

  - **Infinite horizon networking**, in which you build relationships with fascinating people in diverse fields that, on the surface, probably can't help you at all. You're building the connection out of pure interest in them as a person—and over time, who knows? Your paths may converge in surprising ways.

- No asks for a year. Avoid asking new connections for any kind of meaningful favor for at least a year, to take the pressure off the relationship and to ensure they're clear that you're not making friends just to take advantage of them.

- When you join a group, go all in. Choose a handful of organizations where you can go deep, reaching out to fellow members and building connections. As your peers, they're more likely to respond positively to your overtures.

- Every relationship has to be reciprocal. If someone is more powerful or has more status than you, it might feel like you have nothing to offer. Get creative. It really is using someone when all you want is to take from them, so think hard about what you can offer in the relationship, and make it your job to keep digging until you can find it. (Hint: if they're powerful in a certain field, most likely, the place where you can offer something of value is in a different area that's of interest to them, such as tips about your city, or fitness strategies, or advice on starting a podcast if you're a longtime host.)

Section Three

Keeping the Faith

OOXOOO

Here's the thing about playing the long game: at times, it can be lonely, maddening, and unfulfilling. It's worth it in the end; we know that intellectually. But in the moment, it often feels like a complete, humiliating waste of time.

As we've discussed in the previous two sections, it's critical to create more white space in your calendar and mind in order to determine your strategic priorities. And you won't be successful unless you're clear on your goals and how to achieve them. Those aren't necessarily easy to do. But they're forward-looking activities, pointed away from the frustrations of the past and toward a brighter future.

In this final section, we're tackling something that's harder, something that trips up many people on the path of playing the long game: being patient enough to see it through. But when you are patient enough, the rewards can be transformative.

8

Strategic Patience

"Unfortunately, the world has given us so many bad messages about the speed of success," Ron Carucci told me one summer afternoon. "We've all heard the cliché about, 'It takes ten years to be an overnight sensation,' but *it really does*. But we actually don't believe it. We think, 'No, but there are shortcuts.' And when we see people who actually look like they're getting shortcuts, we just want it."

Ron is one of the people that others may accuse of being an overnight success. The head of a boutique consulting firm, within the span of a few years he began writing regularly for *Harvard Business Review* and *Forbes*; gave not one but two TEDx talks, one of which has been viewed more than one hundred thousand times; and gave an author talk at Google. But when he first came to me as a coaching client in 2015, he was frustrated. He was excellent at his craft, and clients raved about him. He was a strong writer and loved sharing his ideas. But no one outside his immediate circle, it seemed, was listening. He was a best-kept secret.

I immediately saw the problem. His writing was prodigious and insightful—but the only places it could be found were his company's blog and newsletter. If you weren't already in his orbit, there was no way you'd ever discover him. So we worked to build out his social media presence, and he looked into writing for high-profile publications. It was a heady time. "When we first started," he recalls, "my first *Forbes* column, my first HBR column, my first tweet, my first LinkedIn follower, my first podcast: there's all that euphoria."

His ideas began to be heard, and recognized, and amplified. One of his early hbr.org articles even went viral, becoming one of the ten most popular of the year. But, as he notes, "the honeymoon goes away quickly." Psychologists call it *hedonic adaptation* when the happiness or excitement we feel about something fades, and we revert to our baseline levels. Getting published regularly in august publications would have seemed like an amazing victory to the Ron of a year or two prior. But now he had different problems to contend with.

"You get four hundred page views on *Forbes*, and you suck," he says. "Or you get ten thousand views, but it wasn't thirty thousand. You get one piece accepted into HBR but not another [and think]: 'Damn, I suck.'" It wasn't his editors telling him these things, of course. His friends and family and clients didn't notice, or care about, the page views. As his coach, I reassured him that it was perfectly normal for some pieces to do better than others: it's all part of the process.

But it's often our internal voices that are the hardest to deal with. "You cast your sense of significance and validation into the hands of so many other people," Ron says, "and forfeit your own agency. [You look at] page views, or likes, or shares—all the vanity metrics. You go to the conference and see who will talk to you and who won't. You have to put down the faulty yardsticks. But they're so addictive."

To almost anyone else's eyes, Ron was succeeding wildly. He'd written well over a hundred articles for *Harvard Business Review* and *Forbes* by the fall of 2019. But it didn't feel like enough, because there was always something else he hadn't done—most notably, write a blockbuster book. But he had a plan. He developed a proposal for *To Be Honest*, an in-depth look at business ethics and why companies and individuals sometimes go astray and how to prevent it. It seemed so clear to him: this would be the culmination of his life's work. And then the rejections started coming in.

"It was terrible, because I was not ready for it," he says. "It sent me into a three- or four-month dark cave. There's an emotional sepsis of self-contempt, and inadequacy, and bad comparisons, and terrible victimhood. . . . And you become angry, you become entitled, you go to a terrible place."

When the Plan Doesn't Work Out

We know that success doesn't happen overnight. And yet. We see others who seem to be doing better or going faster, and we wonder what we're doing wrong. Even when we understand intellectually that there are setbacks and false starts—twelve publishers rejected J. K. Rowling's first *Harry Potter* novel, after all[1]—we still can't believe they're happening to us.

I'm no different. I'd always done well in school, and I admired my college professors. How fantastic to get paid to read, and think, and talk about ideas all day! I was hooked, and decided on a career in academia. I was accepted to a master's program in theological studies at Harvard Divinity School and figured I'd have similar success when it came time to enter a doctoral program.

But that's not how it turned out. I was rejected by every single program I applied to. When I saw the final thin envelope in my mailbox, I was beside myself. I had no plan B. It had never occurred to me that I'd need one.

Today, I teach for Duke University's Fuqua School of Business and Columbia Business School, and I've lectured at top business schools on almost every continent. I wasn't wrong about my initial career choice: I knew I'd enjoy writing and speaking and thinking and interacting with students. And I knew I'd be good at it.

But in any enterprise with gatekeepers—and doctoral programs are certainly one—none of that matters if *they* aren't convinced. Over time, excellence will win out. But in the short term, you may well be turned down, and your skills may go unrecognized. Even in situations with no gatekeeper at all—let's say you've started your own blog or podcast—overnight success is vanishingly rare. You need time to build up an audience, and the perseverance to keep going when it seems like no one is listening or the people in charge think you don't have what it takes.

In the moment, it's impossible to tell whether it's not working or whether it's not working *yet*. We're used to relying on authorities to tell us what "good enough" looks like. But the problem is, they can be wrong.

"It looked so real," Ron said about his book proposal. "The finality of it, the ending of it, looked so real. The world was telling me, 'Don't write this book.'"

Bouncing Back from Rejection

That's how it felt for Anne Sugar, too. She was a successful executive coach, working for major companies and Harvard Business School's executive education programs. She loved writing, even taking online poetry classes for fun. She'd been published in prestigious outlets before, so it seemed like a great challenge when she landed the opportunity to write for a new high-profile publication.

For six months, at night and on weekends and in between her coaching clients, she wrote. She produced articles about issues her clients were facing, like delegation and burnout and creativity, and that she thought other professionals were likely struggling with too. And then one day her editor declared, after Anne had written thirty-five articles for free, that her work wasn't good enough. "We don't think you're innovative," she recalls being told.

"I'll admit it," she says. "I cried." Honestly, who wouldn't?

To snap out of her sadness and self-doubt, Anne called up friends and colleagues who had experienced similar setbacks, to see how they'd recovered. It turns out, one of them hadn't. That colleague told Anne, "I never wrote again." The thought terrified her—that one rejection could derail someone's creative output forever. Anne vowed not to make the same mistake. Within five months, she had started writing for another, equally prestigious business publication. She was back on the horse.

The journey to becoming a recognized expert—or even to getting your ideas heard a bit more—isn't easy. Newbies often worry about online haters: *What if someone attacks you, or doesn't like your ideas?* That's not impossible, but the far more common problem in your first couple of years is actually the opposite: complete and total silence. "There was this echo of 'Is anybody there?' for a really long time," Anne says.

You'll sometimes wonder if anyone is listening, or if your hard work is worth it. Giving a talk or publishing an article or presenting to a client may feel huge for you, but others may barely notice. It can be discouraging. But, as Anne says, with patience, the "raindrops" of recognition do eventually start to fall: "Someone liked one of the *Harvard Business Review* stories I wrote, and that got me an invitation to be on a podcast." She started to get connection requests on LinkedIn from people she didn't know, new subscribers to her email list, and requests to review someone's book. None of these things is evidence of world-beating success. But they provide a clue: others are starting to listen, and they want to hear more.

Anne emailed me recently. She'd just hit her three-year anniversary of making a push around her writing, and "something has been happening to me lately," she said. "Recently, articles I write and posts on LinkedIn have been going viral. In the beginning, I would get about one hundred views [per article] for about two years—and I was excited with that!" But in the past month, one of her LinkedIn posts had received fifty-five thousand views, and a *Forbes* piece got more than fifteen thousand. "I am not doing anything different at all," she said. But over time, she realized, she'd been building up momentum. She'd learned to put it all in perspective. "It's been a long time toiling," she said, "and I have a long way to go."

Seeing those hints and glimmers on the horizon? It feels sweet.

I tell participants in my Recognized Expert course that they have to be willing to do the work of sharing their ideas publicly for at least two or three years before they start to see *any* results. It's a huge leap of faith—so much time invested for a very uncertain outcome. It's easy to see why others wouldn't bother or would quickly give up. But that becomes your competitive advantage.

If you can practice the art of strategic patience—not blindly waiting for good things to magically happen, but understanding the work that needs to be done and *making* it happen—you're far better off than almost anyone else in your realm. The timing varies for everyone, of course. But in my experience, and often for my clients, around two to three years in, you do start to see the "raindrops": the little victories that show you're on the right path.

And by year five, you've opened up an almost insurmountable distance between yourself and the competition. When potential clients type a term into a search engine, it's your articles that come up. When they listen to a podcast about your area of expertise, you're the guest. And when they want to hire a speaker, or a high-level employee, or an expert consultant to advise them—you're the only logical choice.

Exponential Growth

As humans, our minds are great at understanding linear growth: $1 + 1 = 2$.

But we generally have a much harder time grasping the implications of exponential growth, as in the famous story of the king who agreed to an inventor's payment terms: one grain of rice on the first square of a chessboard, two on the second, four on the third, and so on. It sounds rather modest at first. Yet by the time he got to the sixty-fourth and final square, the king owed more than eighteen quintillion grains.[2]

In their book *Bold*, Peter Diamandis and Steven Kotler discuss what they call "exponential technologies"—innovations such as driverless cars, or 3D printing, or artificial intelligence. For a long time, sometimes decades, people dismiss exponential technologies, saying they're overhyped and ineffective. But then, on the back half of the chessboard, they suddenly pop into public consciousness and amaze everyone: *Where did this come from? How did this happen?* They've been there all along, growing and developing. It was just that their early progress, even though it was exponential even then, was too small for the naked eye to perceive.

Diamandis and Kotler call this the "deception phase" of exponential growth:

> This happens because the doubling of small numbers often produces results so miniscule they are often mistaken for the plodder's progress of linear growth. Imagine Kodak's first digital camera with 0.01 megapixels doubling to 0.02, 0.02 to 0.04, 0.04 to 0.08. To the casual observer, these numbers all look like zero. Yet big change is on the horizon. Once these doublings break the whole-number barrier (become 1, 2, 4, 8, etc.), they are only twenty doublings away from a millionfold improvement, and only thirty doublings away from a billionfold improvement. It is at this stage that exponential growth, initially deceptive, starts becoming visibly disruptive.[3]

This makes sense in the world of technology, but it's equally true in the world of business. As Derek Sivers, the music entrepreneur of "hell yeah or no" fame, described in one podcast interview, his company "didn't really take off for four years. . . . Very often I meet people who start their dream idea, and they're a few months into it and they say, 'It's just not going well!' I'm like, 'It's been a few months! Come on!' When I was three years into CD Baby, it was just me and a guy in my house."[4] By year ten, he had sold the company for $22 million.[5]

And it turns out, it's not just technology and business that exponential growth applies to: it's also life. As Aikido master George Leonard notes, "In the land of the quick fix it may seem radical, but to learn anything significant, to make any lasting change in yourself, you must be willing to spend *most* of your time on the plateau, to keep practicing even when it seems you are getting nowhere."[6]

Let's say it again: most of life is spent in the deception phase. And it's not just others who are deceived by outward appearances, questioning our approach or our competency. It's also ourselves. We look at the lack of results, sometimes for years on end, and quite naturally wonder if we're good enough, or if we have what it takes. Playing the long game means being patient enough to wade through that self-doubt and persevere.

But how, exactly, do we do that?

When Things Seem Bleak

Pushing forward, despite rejection or no response at all, is far easier said than done. That's why it's crucial to ask ourselves three key questions that can help keep us on track:

- Why am I doing this?

- How has it worked for others?

- What do my trusted advisers say?

Let's dive into each.

Why Am I Doing This?

It's easy to get caught up in the wrong metrics, so it's essential to get clear on your core principles. "You have to write down, 'This is what I value, this is what I know to be true, this is who I want to be in the world,'" Ron Carucci says.

Being clear on that helps you avoid the false temptation to measure yourself against others. As Ron puts it: "You have to keep that sense of values in front of you at all times, so that when you're triggered with one of those vanity metrics, or your sense of well-being is anxious, or when you feel like you're on uneven footing about, 'That article wasn't accepted,' or 'I didn't get hired for that speech,' or 'That client picked somebody else,' or 'My boss didn't like my idea,' you're ready for that moment."

Your values keep you fortified—and that's something Ron kept in mind as he finally wrote his book. Because, in the end, he did land a deal with a commercial publisher and had the opportunity to work with an editor he loves. He refocused himself on first principles: he wanted to write the book because he has something important to say about ethics at work and how to make the business world a better place. "I'm learning to just enjoy being in this moment, and the privilege that I get to create it."

When you focus on how you're helping others with your ideas, and who you want to be in the world, you're far better able to keep things in perspective.

How Has It Worked for Others?

Do you *actually* know what it takes to succeed?

Most of us don't. And as a result, our expectations can sometimes be way out of line. For the hundreds of professionals I've worked with in my Recognized Expert community, I've noticed a common tendency: they want to revisit their strategy too often. (I used to be just as guilty of this.) They're not seeing results as quickly as they want, so they become restless and want to change focus. *Should I start a podcast? Maybe I should be vlogging! What am I missing? What else should I be doing?*

This creates strategic whiplash, and a scenario where you *never* see results because you're not giving it enough time. What we need to do, instead, is two things that seem simple enough—yet staying disciplined enough to do them is anything but.

The first is to identify role models who have accomplished all or part of what you'd like to. The goal is not just to gawk or admire, but also to study their path deeply so you can understand exactly what they did on their way to success and interrogate whether the same moves are right for you. The second is to get a clear understanding of their timeline so you'll know how long, realistically, it should take for you to show results.

That's the approach David Burkus took. A speaker and the author of books including *The Myths of Creativity* and *Friend of a Friend*, Burkus once interviewed the well-known business thinker Daniel Pink for his podcast. They were chatting after the show, and David mentioned his frustration that his career wasn't advancing as fast as he'd like. As David recounts, Pink "paused for a pretty long beat. And then he goes, 'Well, you've got to remember that you've been doing this for three years, and I've been doing it for twenty. So anything I tell you probably won't work for you, because you really need to just give yourself more time.'"

Pink's answer felt frustrating at the time; David was looking for tactics to implement. "But then you hang up, you think about it more and more and more, and the wisdom of it sets in," he says. "I think you simultaneously have to wrestle with gratitude for what you've managed to get out there and frustration that you haven't gone further. I don't know a single achiever who doesn't experience that constant tension."

So David created his own way to think about the situation: "I am unashamed of jovially referring to myself as the next, *next* Daniel Pink. I say that partly as a joke, partly to position my writing in people's minds with someone they're more familiar with, and partly to remind myself that this is going to take twenty years. I remind myself that while I don't have the results that Dan Pink has in 2020, I do have the results he had in 2001."

Comparison isn't, by itself, a harmful practice. Seeing what others have done can be a way of inspiring ourselves or sparking new ideas. But our comparisons have to be realistic. We can't take a cursory glance at someone's bio and assume that things came quickly or easily for them. When we realize, as David did, that our heroes have a head start of years or decades, it's far easier to be gentle with ourselves and remember that strategic patience and hard work eventually pay off. As David says, "Impatience isn't necessarily a bad thing if it motivates you to work. It's only a bad thing if you tell yourself you're failing."

What Do My Trusted Advisers Say?

When things aren't breaking our way, it's easy to go to a dark place. Every setback seems like a permanent judgment or an inescapable fact. It can be hard, and sometimes even impossible, to dig ourselves out—which is why we need a group of trusted advisers around us. Ideally, they're people who have done the same things you hope to, or who have sufficient insight into the process that they can guide you. We all need general cheerleaders in our lives, such as relatives and friends who think we're great no matter what. But we also want to have a coterie of people whose professional judgment we trust, people who can tell us, "This idea is worth pursuing" or "It might be time to move on."

Creating and sharing new ideas can be a fraught process. Some may be well received, while others are ignored or vilified. The author Seth Godin likes to say about new endeavors, "This might not work." That can feel very risky, both to our emotions and to our sense of professional competence. And that's why you need a kind and wise sounding board.

As Ron Carucci says, "You have to have community around you. You have to have people who will tell you who you are when you lose sight of it." Trusted advisers can help you evaluate whether you're pursuing the right goals, whether your strategy for attaining them seems promising, and whether your timeline is realistic—all things that, in the moment, are incredibly hard for us to judge on our own.

What we need is the ability to pivot and reinvent ourselves when necessary. But changing course means thinking hard about what, exactly, it means to fail.

Remember:

- To gain notice in your field, it often takes two to three years of effort before you see *any* results. At that point, you'll often start to see "raindrops"—small, intermittent signs of progress.

- To truly become a recognized expert, it often takes at least five years of consistent effort.

- When things seem bleak, reconnect with your purpose and your strategy by asking yourself:

  - Why am I doing this?

  - How has it worked for others?

  - What do my trusted advisers say?

9

Rethink Failure

It's easy to say "Try new things!" or "Take risks!" But the reality is that we'd all like to be successful *all the time*. Every setback stings.

In 2019, I decided it was time to set some audacious goals for myself:

- Coauthor a book with a famous writer, dramatically raising my profile

- Successfully option the rights to my favorite movie and turn it into a musical as part of the BMI Workshop

- Launch a column for one of the world's most prominent media outlets

- Speak at a particular high-profile industry conference

- Land on the Thinkers50 list of the top business thinkers in the world

This wasn't wishful thinking or cutting out collages to put on a vision board. All of them were stretch goals, but they were plausible if I made the effort. So I set to work.

The Book

I met with the famous author, who loved my idea for a joint project. I'd need to do the legwork and all the writing, but that's what I had expected. With his blessing, I went off and spent several months working on a book proposal. We met up again, I captured his notes and edits in order to make revisions, and then I got to work on our sample chapter. "I'll be done by March," I said, "and if it looks good to you, we can start shopping it to publishers." But when March came and the sample chapter was ready, something wasn't quite right.

"This is really good!" he enthused. But in the interim, he'd had an offer he couldn't refuse—a *million-dollar* advance for another book. Our project, much more modest in scope, would never get that kind of money. I couldn't blame him—of course he should take the million dollars!

But there wasn't much point to doing this project without him. Hundreds of hours of my life went up in smoke.

The Musical

Growing up in a small town in North Carolina, pre-internet, there weren't a lot of windows into the outside world. I watched television and the blockbuster films that came to our local cinema. But generally, it was entertainment for the least common denominator—cartoon sketches of life, masquerading as the real thing.

So when I discovered independent film as a young teenager—once in a great while, one of those films made its way to our local video store—I was enthralled. A certain movie stayed with me for years: a small, poignant coming-of-age story about a group of friends, shot for a mere $210,000.

The moment I entered the BMI musical theater workshop and learned that our second-year project would be adapting another work of art—such as a novel or movie—into a musical, I thought: *this is my chance.* The director, now nearly seventy, wasn't easy to reach. He didn't even have a website. But after some detective work, I hunted down what I thought—maybe, possibly—was his email address. I wrote him a note and waited. Two weeks later, a reply popped into my inbox. "I will be in the US East Coast from Monday, so perhaps we could discuss by phone or Skype when you have a moment," he wrote.

That led to an in-person meeting with him and my composing partner and—miraculously!—an agreement. Instead of simply licensing his work, he wanted to collaborate, so I'd have the chance to work directly with one of my idols. We snapped a selfie to celebrate.

Getting in touch as the project moved forward wasn't easy, since he was shooting in South America and France. My composer and I had spent hours mapping out a plan to make the plotline work as a musical—song placement, hooks, and more. When we finally had a call with the filmmaker, he was on holiday in rural Maine, where cell service feared to tread. He couldn't hear what we said, we repeated it endlessly, and finally we gave up.

The crackly call didn't clarify much. But one thing that came through loud and clear was his dismay at our suggestion to combine two characters into one. In a musical, there are only so many characters, and his cast was large. And, apparently, sacrosanct.

He grew quiet after that. I had to follow up multiple times on each email. My composing partner and I had to move forward, though, if we were going to meet our program deadlines. So we started writing music, pouring more hours into the project.

A month later, the hammer fell. "Congratulations on this lovely theme melody—it's terrific and strikes just the right note," he wrote. But a musical wasn't in the cards after all. His film, he wrote, "seems to me much more suited to being a straight play. . . . Sorry to have led you down this path."

The chance to work with my cinematic hero wasn't going to happen, either.

The Column

I've loved newspapers all my life. Some of my fondest childhood memories were the days when my mother would run errands after picking me up at school. She'd drop me off at the sandwich shop in the strip mall, where I'd order a soda and a meatball sub and contentedly read the newspaper until she was finished.

My first job out of graduate school was as a reporter at the *Boston Phoenix*, a storied alternative newsweekly that launched the careers of superstars like *New Yorker* staff writer Susan Orlean, former *Time* magazine columnist and *Primary Colors* author Joe Klein, and former Clinton administration senior adviser Sidney Blumenthal. Despite getting laid off from that job in 2001—my first hint of the industry decimation that was to come[1]—I retained a reverence for the news. So in October 2018, when I got a call from a colleague who was a reporter at an august newspaper, I was ecstatic. His outlet was planning a new business column: Would I be interested in trying out?

Heading to dinner in Durham, North Carolina, where I was teaching at Duke University, I tried to keep my voice calm as the traffic whizzed past. *What sort of samples would they need? What was the deadline?* For days afterward, all I could think about was how to vanquish my unknown competitors. I was going to write the smartest, funniest, most incisive column ever.

The next weekend, I was going to a wedding. Still putting the finishing touches on my prose, I kept handing my laptop to my then-girlfriend as she got dressed, imploring her to double-check my copy. It had to be just right.

A few weeks later, though, my friend had to pass along the bad news. "Thank you again for this great submission, and for all the hard work you put into it," he wrote me. "Editors here really liked it, but ultimately decided to go in a different direction, at least for now." He held out a sliver of hope, though: "Your name was very much in the mix, and we hope that we might be able to circle back with you in the future, depending on how this project plays out."

Were they letting me down easy and just being nice? Or did they mean it?

I dropped my friend's editor a note about six months later to check in. He told me to check back later that summer, so I did. He said he'd be in touch, and he wasn't. So I followed up again and again ("Moving this to the top of your inbox!") every few weeks. I wasn't going to throw away my shot.

Finally, a year had passed. The editor invited me to submit yet another sample column, so I did. I'd now written nearly four thousand words for them. They'd gotten an awfully good look at me. And upon further reflection, they still didn't like what they saw.

"Hi Dorie," the editor wrote. "I wanted to let you know that we've decided to go with another candidate. I thought your sample was strong. . . . But I want to keep the voice of the column a bit more irreverent."

Oh. Would there be another chance in the offing? Another way they could make use of my talents?

"Thanks again for participating," he wrote me back. "I hope you'll keep reading."

Apparently not.

The Talk

Six months before the final newspaper rejection, I submitted a video application to speak at a top industry conference. Over the years, I'd built up a robust keynote speaking business and was often paid well to give talks. But this conference represented a personal goal for me. It was unpaid but high visibility, and I wanted it.

The website hadn't been clear about the timeline for decision-making, so I tried to be patient. When a colleague who had also applied was turned down, I was encouraged—not because of his rejection, but because I viewed it as a sign that my application was still in play and would surely be accepted soon. But months passed. The conference started to announce speakers, but not all of them—a few at a time, with more announcements coming at an unspecified future date. I knew someone on the selection committee. He couldn't tell me anything official, but *unofficially*, they liked my video. They were still deciding.

The date of the conference loomed. *Should I buy a ticket?* I wanted to attend regardless, but it would be redundant if I were accepted to speak. Would it jinx the process if I waited in hopes of an imminent invitation? I finally caved in and paid for the ticket.

Just weeks before the conference, the final lineup was announced: I wasn't on it. They'd never even bothered to respond to my application. Not long after, I went out to dinner with some friends. "Do you ever get the feeling," I asked, "that sometimes *nothing is working?*"

The List

By that point in the year, it was November. Four of the five major aspirations I'd had for 2019 had—clearly and decisively—failed. I'd chosen audacious goals deliberately; I knew not all of them would pan out. But at least *some* would—right? I was beginning to lose hope.

I'd already bought my plane ticket to London to attend Thinkers50, the biennial conclave of the world's top business thinkers— the one that Nihar Chhaya attended and wrote about for *Forbes.* Previously I'd been a Thinkers50 "thinker to watch," but that wouldn't necessarily translate into making it onto the coveted list. The people on that list were business giants, like W. Chan Kim and Renée Mauborgne, whose seminal book *Blue Ocean Strategy* has sold four million copies. On a chilly Monday evening, I found myself in a cavernous banquet hall with a sea of tuxes and ball gowns surrounding me. The evening's program started, and a list of names flashed on the screen.

Mine was on it. That evening, six weeks before year's end, I was named one of the top 50 business thinkers in the world.

It took eleven years and three books. It took four successive dashed dreams that year, and being rejected repeatedly. But it happened.

Sometimes our bets pay off, and sometimes they don't. We have to make them anyway. Success is about being excellent at what you do. But, inevitably, there's a subjective element. The editor thought my writing was strong, but it just wasn't what he was looking for.

You have to be excellent *and* you need at bats. Because in the short term, you may be rejected for a million reasons that have nothing to do with you. In the long term, though, the statistics are on your side: success comes when you make enough attempts.

But in the midst of failure, and setbacks, and the sinking feeling that it may *never* work out, how do you keep pushing through?

The Silicon Valley Strategy

Entrepreneur and Stanford professor Steve Blank saw what was happening around him in Silicon Valley. Eager entrepreneurs, high on venture capital funding, would hire massive teams and burn through vast sums of money. But many of them discovered that their amazing plans, concocted in the basements and garages of startup lore, didn't turn out to be so great once they hit the marketplace. It's not that the products didn't work. They did—perfectly!

The problem was, no one seemed to want them in the first place. Creators were operating in a vacuum, putting in the time to make something perfect before they had even validated that it was a thing they should be spending their time on. The antidote, Blank realized, was placing small bets: creating a "minimum viable product" that wasn't very fancy or impressive, but showed what you were trying to do.

If customers were interested—if they were willing to download it or use it or maybe even pay for it—that was evidence that there was something there, and you could safely start allocating your time to make it better. But if no one bit? Best to just move on, so you didn't waste time or money or energy. Blank's concepts, popularized in a 2011 book by Eric Ries, eventually became known as the lean startup methodology.

This simple philosophy—test before you fully invest—took Silicon Valley by storm, making processes there far more efficient. But it turns out, it's also applicable in our own lives.

All too often, smart professionals hesitate to put their "thing"—whether it's an article, a new website, a talk, an idea—out into the world. "It's not quite ready yet," they'll say, or "I'm still making a few tweaks," or "It needs a little more time." That's fine up to a point; you don't want to release something into the world that's awful, or so rough that it's unintelligible. But after a while, this kind of thinking becomes an excuse that can hold us back.

The lesson we can learn from Silicon Valley and the lean startup methodology is that we should, in the early days, treat *everything* as an experiment. Failure is upsetting to so many of us because it implies finality: you tried to accomplish something, and it didn't happen. But an experiment, which you recognize from the beginning has an uncertain outcome, can hardly be called a failure. You know it'll take multiple iterations to get the result you want, and you set your expectations accordingly. As Thomas Edison is supposed to have said, it's finding 999 ways *not* to invent the light bulb. You haven't failed—you've gotten data that helps you refine your approach so you can succeed in the future.

Multiple Paths

Acting, says Dayna Del Val, "was all I ever wanted to do." Growing up in a small town in North Dakota, "I did my first play when

I was six and I never, ever turned back." A college theater major who wowed her department, she left the day after graduation for Utah to perform summer stock with her best friend. After that, they'd move to Los Angeles, and Dayna would launch her Hollywood career. Everything was proceeding according to plan—until a week later, when Dayna learned she was pregnant.

"Nothing that devastating has ever happened in my life," she recalls. "There was no way I was going to be a single mom and move to Los Angeles. Everything I thought I wanted, everything I thought I had worked for, was immediately done."

Sometimes even our most cherished dreams come up short. So what do we do then?

When her son was in fifth grade, Dayna thought about taking a one-year sabbatical from her teaching job and moving to Los Angeles, just as a trial. But then she visited the LA schools, which were underfunded and overburdened. "It felt so unfair to ask him to sacrifice his one childhood for my dream," she thought. Then she played it out even further. "I thought, 'OK, let's say this dream happens," she says. "Let's say I get cast, and I have to be on set at 4 a.m. Who's going to take care of my nine-year-old at 4 a.m.? I don't know anybody out here. I couldn't make it work, so I didn't. I came home."

Her dream, it seemed, was dead. After all, the border of North Dakota and Minnesota wasn't exactly Hollywood East. But a part of her wondered: Might there be a way to channel some of her creative energy?

It turns out, there was. She started to try out for regional acting gigs in Minneapolis—and nailed her auditions. She did voiceover work for a half-dozen local banks and a major hospital system. Eventually, she landed a signature role, becoming "the face of North Dakota" in the state's tourism campaign. "Sometimes I was biking across bridges in Valley City," she recalls. "Sometimes I was hiking in the Badlands of Medora. Sometimes I was shopping in Fargo. I have been on the cover of the hunting and fishing guide, like, seven years in a row." She adds, "Believe me, I don't hunt or fish. It's why it's called acting."

Dayna's visibility as an actor led to something else unexpected: a job offer. The Arts Partnership was a small nonprofit advocating for 150 arts-related nonprofits and businesses near the North Dakota–Minnesota border. Might Dayna like to run it? For the next decade, she served as its executive director, heading up fundraising, communication, and arts advocacy in the region. "In ten years, I quadrupled the budget," she says.

In the end, Dayna never made it to Los Angeles—though as it happens, her son, now in his twenties, lives there (he's an engineer, not an actor). But Dayna's experience illustrates another important principle when it comes to persevering through setbacks: we have to realize there are multiple paths to our goals. She didn't "fail" because she didn't become the next Meryl Streep. She found her own way to become an actor and enhance the arts for an entire community. "I had a way bigger career than many of my friends who moved to New York or Los Angeles," she says. They often spent years enduring rejection, never getting to do the work they loved, while she thrived in the local creative ecosystem.

If Hollywood came calling today, Dayna says, of course she'd go. But she's not waiting for it. She's created a life she loves. She started teaching a course on entertainment entrepreneurship at her alma mater, Minnesota State University Moorhead. She's working on a screenplay and exploring ways to share her ideas through speaking and writing. Post-pandemic, she says: "Who cares where you're located today? You and I could be next door, or we could be in New York and Fargo, and it doesn't matter."

Your original plan may not work out. No matter how brilliant or qualified you are, life may get in the way, or you may not be chosen. Maybe you desperately wanted a job at Apple, and it didn't work out. If you let that rejection stymie you permanently, then yes—it is "failure."

But maybe that experience can become a lever to consider other opportunities. Maybe you can land a job with one of the company's big tech competitors—or even a brilliant, design-forward startup that could become the *next* Apple. Maybe you start a research project to better understand Apple's methodology, which could become an article or a book or a graduate thesis.

When you measure yourself entirely based on factors outside your control, like a random person's decision to hire you or not, it can be devastating to fall short. But if you simultaneously nurture several paths to your desired outcome, you're not only taking back power from arbitrary gatekeepers, you're also forcing yourself to think more creatively.

As Dayna's experience shows, there are multiple ways to reach your goal.

Search for Alternatives

A few years ago, I floated an idea to participants in my newly created Recognized Expert community: Would they be interested in a mastermind group? Masterminds, first popularized by Napoleon Hill in the 1920s and 1930s, are small groups of people that meet regularly in order to talk about challenges and opportunities in their business, and receive advice from peers who have gotten to know them over time. I loved the concept of assembling and running a group: together, we could help each member level up their success.

But would anyone be interested in this as a paid program? There was only one way to find out. I sent a message to members, and waited. Encouragingly, four people wrote back and expressed interest: not bad for one email!

One of the challenges of a mastermind, though, is making sure you have the right mix of people. Unlike many online courses, where people consume information on their own, or even regular classrooms, where the professor is the main attraction and discussion is minimal, masterminds are crucially dependent on the interaction between participants. You can't have someone with a million-dollar company next to someone who just launched their business yesterday—the concerns, questions, and insights will be vastly different, and they won't really be able to help one another effectively. You have to curate the right group.

Accordingly, the first question you face when you launch a mastermind is a version of the classic chicken-and-egg conundrum: *Who else is in the group?* You have no idea, because you're just forming the group, but many people won't commit until they have validation that "their type of person" will be in the room. My four interested parties quickly dropped to two, because I didn't yet have enough information to promise who the other participants would be.

I could have dropped the idea of a mastermind altogether. Certainly, it wouldn't have been worth it to run the program with just two people. Perhaps I should wait until I had a larger following. But instead, I decided to ask two questions: How can I salvage this concept? And is there a way I could reconfigure it so that it *does* work?

I had conversations with the two people who were interested and asked a lot of questions about their businesses, how they wanted to develop, and what they wanted to learn. Then, instead of creating a traditional mastermind, I proposed something new: a bespoke experience for just the two of them, tailored to their personal learning agendas. They'd come to New York, and the three of us would have time together to strategize in depth about their businesses. And because they were both interested in professional speaking, we'd take a road trip. They'd accompany me on a speaking engagement, watching me in action as I prepared and delivered the speech, networked with the hosts, and more, and I could explain everything to them in an ongoing play-by-play. It was a different sort of experience—one they were delighted to sign up for, and one that also worked for me because it piggybacked on my existing activities.

The arrangement served as a valuable learning experience. Even if you've built up a strong brand, it's hard to convince people to pay for something new: they aren't sure what it'll be like, or if they'll enjoy it. And they may not be fully confident you can deliver the promised results.

The year I spent running the modified mastermind laid the groundwork for the rollout of a more traditional group, with nine participants, the next year. Subsequently, masterminds have become a healthy revenue stream for me, and a way to help great colleagues grow their business outside of my typical one-on-one coaching. But it never would have been possible if I'd thrown away the mastermind concept after meeting initial reluctance and seeing that it was harder to pull together than I'd imagined.

Similarly, I was crushed when the well-known author decided he wouldn't be able to collaborate with me on the book project.

It was so many months wasted after pulling together a complete book proposal and sample chapter. But I later scraped through the material and identified several articles I could write based on the research I'd conducted, ensuring that the ideas would nonetheless get out there and that I'd derive some professional benefit from it.

As I learned, you always have to ask: *Might there be an alternative way I can still use this?*

Precommitment: Put a Date on It

"For decades, I had associated a full calendar with financial stability," says Sam Horn, an author and consultant. "It was a measure of my success." And that's exactly what she'd optimized for, until one day a few years ago.

"I was in Laguna Beach, California," she recalls, "and I'd just finished two very intense days of consults. And I drove my rental car to the airport, and I was sitting there, and my son Andrew called. And he sensed something in my voice and he said, 'What's up?' And I said, 'I'm so exhausted I don't even know if I can get on that plane tonight.'"

Andrew paused for a moment. "Mom, there's something about you I don't understand," he told her. "You're an entrepreneur. You run your own business. You can do pretty much anything you want to. And you're not taking advantage of it." He convinced her not to get on the plane. Then he called the hotel she had just left and extended her stay by several days: she needed a break. "And that night, instead of being on a red-eye back home, flying back and forth, I'm listening to the ocean in my ears," Sam recalls.

With that small opening, she gave herself space to realize she had a dream that she'd been pushing off for years: she wanted to live by the water. This wasn't the typical dream of a lake house or an oceanfront property. She wanted to spend an entire year of self-discovery moving from location to location, but always by the water. Most critical, she gave herself a deadline to act: October 1.

"Whatever it is," says Sam, "whether someone wants to write a book, launch their own business, travel on their own, or whatever, I'll just say almost unequivocally: if you do not have a date on the calendar, it is not getting done. Because life will intervene and you'll say, 'OK, well, not now, later.' And then you set up that loop." Sam's quest led her to swim with dolphins in Florida and whales in Maui, and to dive fully clothed into Walden Pond. She even wrote a book about her experiences, called *Someday Is Not a Day in the Week*.

Fulfilling your goals, even dearly held ones, isn't easy. Sam ran into plenty of obstacles on the path to her year by the water, from incredulous friends ("Sam, are you sick?") to fears that her business would suffer if she went on the road. "Yet it happened," she says, "because I circled October 1 on my calendar and made a vow to be out the door on that day." Her biggest lesson? "A precommitment needs to have metrics if it's going to succeed."

Involve Your Community

One precommitment strategy is naming a date. Another, it turns out, is involving other people.

Kim Cantergiani was a C-suite leader at a disability services organization, not to mention a wife and busy mom. Between her job and her family, there were always pressing needs. What ended up falling through the cracks, inevitably, was her health. Finally—"a size 22 and 191 pounds, with countless failed weight-loss programs behind me"—she decided she'd had enough. She knew willpower alone wasn't going to cut it; she'd tried that route before and failed.

Leveraging the power of community, Kim found her own way to hold herself accountable. She created a "pound-a-thon" campaign, in which she tapped friends, family, and neighbors to pledge a donation to the local battered women's shelter for each pound she lost. Now, if she failed in her dieting quest, she'd be letting down more than just herself. "I couldn't possibly be seen in public with a candy bar and Dr. Pepper after that," she says. Her weight-loss campaign was so successful, she was featured in *People* magazine and went on to become a personal trainer and opened her own weight-loss and fitness studio.

Every successful professional who wants to chart a new course or aim for a big opportunity will, sometimes, hit a wall. And in moments of irrational emotion, like the kind of self-doubt brought on by failure, we simply can't trust ourselves. It's too easy to get discouraged, indulge in self-blame, and take rash actions. We may be tempted to give up entirely or to switch our strategy to whatever fad seems promising in the moment. We can't afford to get derailed prematurely—so it's important to plan in advance for the setbacks we're likely to encounter so we can overcome them. We can put a date on the calendar, knowing it'll be much harder to back out, and enlist the support of friends and colleagues, knowing we'll be ashamed to slack off when they're counting on us.

Most goals, if they're big enough, probably *will* fail. If you reach every single goal you set, you're probably aiming too low. The secret is ensuring we're not paralyzed by failure or sent into a tailspin. We have to look for alternatives, because there are almost always other paths. A full two years after my failed book proposal, I was able to repurpose the concepts into an online course that is likely to be far more lucrative than the book itself would have been.

Obstacles are inevitable. In order to succeed, you have to learn how to climb above them, dig beneath them, smash them to pieces, or simply go around: your choice.

The one thing you can't do is give up.

Remember:

- You need to be excellent at what you do. But you also need at bats, because random chance means that even excellent performers will "fail" sometimes. You have to give yourself multiple chances to succeed, because over time, if you're truly top-notch, you will.

- Test out concepts and ideas in small ways before investing fully. That way, if something doesn't work, it's not failure—it's an experiment, and you learned something valuable from it.

- Always think broadly and identify multiple paths to your goal. One might not work out, but there are almost always other possibilities.

- Try to adapt plans that didn't work out. Are there alternative ways you can leverage the connections you made, the time you put in, or the work you created?

- To make success more likely, always put a date on the calendar and involve others in your plan. That enhances your level of seriousness and commitment.

10

Reap the Rewards

"I could have written that *way* better."

"Why did *she* get the promotion?"

"I can't believe people are paying to listen to *that guy*."

In our culture, it's hard to get away from comparison. H. L. Mencken, the famed early twentieth-century satirist, defined wealth as "any income that is at least one hundred dollars more a year" than what your brother-in-law makes. But these days, it's not just our brothers-in-law that we're comparing ourselves to. It's our colleagues at work, our friends from high school and college, reality TV stars, influencers, and anyone else whose social media feed crosses our sight lines.

In other words, it's everyone.

I once attended a one-woman show—*Lezzie with a Z,* a nod to Liza Minnelli's *Liza with a "Z"*—by Caitlin Lee Reid, a talented performer who shared the story of her dream, ultimately unsuccessful, to make it on Broadway. Life was pretty good, though: she had a wonderful voice, a job in the tech world she enjoyed, and she was happily married to a beautiful wife, thanks in part to her friend Stefani, who years before had encouraged Caitlin to come out publicly.

The only catch is that Stefani, as it happened, was Stefani Germanotta—otherwise known as Lady Gaga. It's bad enough to compare ourselves with our brother-in-law. It's very, very hard to compare yourself to a friend who has had six albums top the Billboard charts and is one of the world's best-known pop stars.[1]

Caitlin navigated her journey with wit and grace, but doing so isn't easy. Playing the long game becomes a painful challenge when it feels like others are advancing and we aren't. It can feel shameful not to have all the answers, or not to be the best, or not to be as far along as we'd hoped or imagined.

The first week of my BMI musical theater workshop, they paired me with a composer to work on a song: my first assignment! Up until then, the only songs I'd written had been burnished with the encouragement of my supportive coach. The truth was, I still didn't exactly know what I was doing. I found myself in the program with two composers who had master's degrees in musical theater, while I was a complete novice. Everyone else seemed to have their own bevy of credentials: this one had graduated from Northwestern University's lauded musical theater program and had written the annual revue; that one had won almost every musical theater fellowship in Canada; another was a professor of music theory at a university.

The composer I was matched with for my first assignment was no rookie, either. She had already completed a Los Angeles–based program similar to BMI's—and just to be versatile, she'd gone through that one as a lyricist. In short, she knew how to do my job better than I did. My first lyrics to her were a shambles; it seemed impossible to tease out where and how to add words to the electronic riff I received. So she stepped in to help. But I felt like an idiot, and I'm fairly sure she thought I was one.

During the workshop's first year, they rotate you to work with a different composer every few weeks. My next one, a great musician, wasn't a native English speaker and thankfully just seemed glad I could throw in some words that made sense. By then, I'd quickly absorbed the most basic lessons about what I needed to do. But the sting of humiliation, and the judgment I was sure I felt emanating from that first composer, left its mark. I'd spent two full years working to get accepted into the program, and it became quite clear: my journey wasn't over. It had barely begun, and I was already behind.

At points like these, it's easy to give up. We say to ourselves, *Maybe I don't have what it takes,* or *I'll never be good enough, so why bother?* It's also easy to get vengeful or entitled: *These people don't appreciate true talent!* Or, *the system is rigged!* Or, *I'm not going to play their stupid games.*

Long-term thinking, and the actions that enable your eventual success, requires sacrifice—including, at times, the sacrifice of our dignity and pride. If you're willing to endure the discomfort and humiliation, the rewards can be powerful.

But most people aren't.

Of Marshmallows and Men

You've probably heard of Walter Mischel's famous "marshmallow study," conducted at Stanford University's Bing Nursery School in the 1960s. Children were given an option: have one delicious treat right now (marshmallows were an option), or wait fifteen minutes—alone in the room with the treat—and get two. The kicker came decades later, when the children's study results were matched up against their life outcomes. It turned out that the children who had the self-control and self-possession to wait performed markedly better on almost every measure. As *New Yorker* writer Maria Konnikova put it, a child who could wait longer "would perform better academically, earn more money, and be healthier and happier. She would also be more likely to avoid a number of negative outcomes, including jail time, obesity, and drug use."[2]

That much, if you enjoy reading social science or pop business literature, is well known. But the crucial point, which is often missed, is this: you're not simply one type of person forever, either a Cookie Monster gobbling treats or a diligent saint. All of us can learn to delay gratification and enhance our self-control. In other words, all of us can become long-term thinkers.

When it comes to resisting short-term temptations (I'm going to eat that piece of cake or have a second drink), the trick is to "cool" the impulse by, as Konnikova recounts, "putting the object at an imaginary distance (a photograph isn't a treat) or by reframing it (picturing marshmallows as clouds, not candy). Focusing on a completely unrelated experience can also work, as can any technique that successfully switches your attention."

That's great for avoiding extra pounds. But the process is obviously a bit different for forcing ourselves to do workplace activities that are important in the long term—write articles, study for an extra certification, attend a networking event—but feel painful or burdensome in the moment. Is there a way we can train ourselves to do what's necessary, the things that we claim we want most?

In fact, there is. The secret may simply be to get started—in a *very small* way. The problem with writing a book or learning a new skill is that it often feels so monumental, it's overwhelming. How can you ever sit down and write three hundred pages? The answer, of course, is you can't: you break it down into smaller pieces.

But for someone who hasn't written a book before, or feels an aversion to the process, even willing yourself to write a chapter may be too much. That's why Stanford psychologist BJ Fogg has a different approach. "When a behavior is easy, you don't need to rely on motivation," he says.[3] His recommendation, then, is that we should strive to create "tiny habits" that are so miniscule and doable that they're impossible to resist. When Fogg wanted to create a flossing habit for himself, he decided to floss just one tooth. Because getting started is often the hard part, once you're flossing that one tooth, it becomes far easier to keep going and floss them all. Similarly, he suggests getting in the habit of paying *one* bill or tidying *one* item on your desk.

For any activity where you feel nervous or averse, find one small way to begin. You don't have to reconnect with your entire Rolodex; just email one long-lost friend. You don't have to sit down and write an entire novel; just hammer out one paragraph.

The key is getting started.

Over the course of this book, we've talked about the foundational skills necessary to become a long-term thinker: a willingness to say no, because you'll never achieve your own agenda if you don't have room to set one in the first place; a willingness to "fail," understanding that what most people call failure is simply useful data you're gathering; and a willingness to trust in the process long enough to see results.

Now it's time to put these strategies into practice so you can master them in your own life.

Understand What It Takes

Jeff Bezos, in his 2018 letter to Amazon shareholders, tells an unusual story about handstands. "A close friend recently decided to learn to do a perfect free-standing handstand," he recounted.[4] She took a handstand workshop at a yoga studio, but wasn't progressing as fast as she wanted, so she hired—yes!—a handstand coach.

Bezos recounts what the coach told her: "Most people think that if they work hard, they should be able to master a handstand in about two weeks. The reality is that it takes about six months of daily practice. If you think you should be able to do it in two weeks, you're just going to end up quitting."

Far too many of us are like Bezos's overoptimistic friend. We never bother to research the process or what it really takes to succeed. We let ourselves run with a vision of unicorns and rainbows, overlooking the hard work and sacrifice that would have been apparent—if only we'd taken the time to look. Inevitably, disappointment follows.

We can make ourselves smarter and more resilient if, from the outset, we truly make the effort to understand what success looks like. How have other people done it? What does it require, in general? It's possible that you may develop a better or smarter way to succeed, but that should be a pleasant surprise, not your up-front expectation. If it takes everyone else three years to make something happen, don't assume you can knock it out in six months.

Distance to Empty

Back in chapter 1, we met Dave Crenshaw, whose college classmate derided Dave's intention to create work-life balance, and told him he'd have to sacrifice his family in order to build a lucrative career. More than twenty years later, Dave—who has built a successful business, works thirty hours a week and takes two months off per year—has had the last laugh. How, precisely, did he manage it?

The secret, he says, is your "distance to empty." Think about a car. These days, many have a feature that tells you how many miles you can drive until you're out of gas. It's the same for entrepreneurs or other professionals: "How many days can you step away from what you're doing and it still operates?" Dave says. Have you put in place the systems you need so that the business doesn't collapse if you're not working 24/7?

A common mistake for overworked professionals is to aim too big, too fast. We hear that Dave takes off two months a year and immediately want to jump onboard. *Why can't I do that too?* But it's overambitious and impractical: we need to understand our own current "distance to empty" and work to expand that strategically. I remember freaking out during one summer trip to the Adirondacks when I discovered that the cellular service was so spotty, I couldn't reliably download emails. I insisted on driving into town each day so I could check my messages. My distance to empty at that point was, apparently, about 18 hours: not very impressive.

Start by looking at your "finish line," Dave suggests. "It's defining the time in your day at which you will stop. If you're not able to stop at a consistent time each day, you're not ready for the marathon." If you're knocking off at 7:30 p.m. every night, see if you can roll it back to 7 p.m., and eventually 6:30 p.m. It's like resetting your circadian rhythms: if you're a night owl, you could certainly force yourself to wake up at 6 a.m. one day. But you'll collapse from fatigue, and the practice won't stick. Instead, you need to adjust gradually.

You have to be firm about it: *I am going to stop work. No matter what is going on in my day, I will stop.* As Dave notes, "You'll encounter things that you can't complete within that time. So, you have to start making choices. Either I'm going to start saying no to things that are low value, or I'm going to have to start developing systems." That forced decision-making makes you better and sharper.

Once you've honed your ability to stop work at a certain time every day, you can start to create what Dave calls an "oasis" in your week, which gives you a small break and ability to reset. "Is it an hour every Friday? Is it half a day?" Dave says. In his case, he takes a break every workday to watch short comedy videos. Even if it's been a fast-paced, stressful day, he knows he has that respite awaiting him. "You commit to it, and you ask yourself strategic questions. 'What must I do to make this happen?' When you start asking questions like that, it improves your manner of thinking and you start to become more effective in your career. You have to look for systemic improvements."

Finally, he says, you can apply the "oasis" concept throughout the year: how can you take off a week, or two weeks, or even a month? Stepping away from work for that long may feel confronting for hard-charging professionals (especially Americans, who aren't used to long breaks). But taking that break forces process improvements that make you, and your business, better. Someone thinking entrepreneurially, Dave says, will realize that "if I do this, I will make more money. I will increase the value of my time."

Getting to take a month off, much less two, may feel impossible. And it probably is, if you're looking at your calendar for next month. But, Dave says, "you have to commit to it well in advance so that all of the choices that you're making with your time and your priorities are around it. That's the problem that a lot of people run into. They're like, 'Oh, I can't do this because I've got this next week, and this next week.' Then think further out. Think three, four months out in the future."

Dave's advice isn't just for planning vacations and taking time off. It's for accomplishing anything meaningful that we want to do. If we blame our full calendars and say we can't possibly write that screenplay or launch that podcast or attend that conference, we may technically be *right*. But we're also being shortsighted. Because we can always make room for what's important if we plan far enough out.

Playing the long game means being willing to think ahead, and even make short-term sacrifices, to accomplish what matters. When we become disciplined about time management, and work relentlessly to enhance our distance to empty, we're giving ourselves the space we need to achieve our dreams.

The Seven-Year Horizon

Jeff Bezos's philosophy is the opposite of the "handstand folly," in which people take on hard tasks under the misguided impression that they'll be easy. Instead, Bezos actively seeks opportunities to take on hard long-term tasks that scare everyone else away. "If everything you do needs to work on a three-year time horizon," he told *Wired* magazine in 2011, "then you're competing against a lot of people. But if you're willing to invest on a seven-year time horizon, you're now competing against a fraction of those people, because very few companies are willing to do that. Just by lengthening the time horizon, you can engage in endeavors that you could never otherwise pursue."[5]

Most of us, truth be told, aren't ambitious enough. Sure, we may spout wild dreams—I have multiple friends who have announced that they want to be Oprah one day. But when it comes to making concrete plans to actualize that, we get timid.

For years, I'd been urging one friend to fulfill his entrepreneurial ambitions and leave his job. One day, he called me up with an announcement: he was finally going to do it!

"Fantastic!" I replied. "When's your last day?"

"Well," he said, "I want to make sure my organization is in a good place before I leave. So I've decided I'll be stepping down in five years." I literally laughed out loud. Chastened, he left for real two months later and started a successful business. But like him, many of us erect unnecessary barriers and don't recognize the enormous progress we can make over time if we just get started.

We also live in terror that our plans may change. *What if I'm wrong? What if it doesn't work out?* None of us has perfect information. Over time and through experience, you may well learn new things about yourself and your skills and preferences, or about the business. You certainly don't have to hew to the same plan for seven years, no matter what. But engaging in long-term planning enables you to think big and adapt where necessary.

In chapter 5, we met Albert DiBernardo, the former engineering executive who, through seeing a friend's post on Facebook, learned about the field of executive coaching and decided to get certified himself. Several years into his retirement career, though, his focus has shifted. "I don't see where the final point is," he says.

"I thought it was coaching, but I am so far from that destination now." He still loves working with clients, but it's just one modality. He conducts workshops, he serves on a corporate board, he invests in real estate, and more. "I'm finding that I seek wisdom," he says. "That's my journey, that's my arc. I'm discovering things about myself still. That's the beauty of this journey."

When you plan for the long term, and are willing to adjust and adapt, you can create extraordinary experiences.

Savor the Process

In early 2019, I got an email—tentative and polite. *Was I free on the 19th of May? And would I consider being the graduation speaker for Mary Baldwin University?*

I was stunned. I had no idea they even knew who I was. But Mary Baldwin, in tiny Staunton, Virginia, is where I spent my freshman and sophomore years of college, at its early college entrance program, more than two decades prior. It's also where I'd met my first girlfriend and scrapped with the college's then-president about forming the university's first LGBT student group (she didn't want me to, but couldn't stop me) and amending the college's nondiscrimination policy (the school finally changed it years later under a welcoming new president, Pamela Fox).

My answer to their question was yes. I spoke at graduation and eagerly accepted an invitation a few months later to join the board of trustees. I travel too much for work already, and I didn't especially need to add four more trips to Virginia to my annual itinerary. But to me, being back on campus, walking those halls again, and seeing how far I'd come—this was the very definition of success. Joining the board of another college would have been a nice honor, but it wouldn't have had the same emotional resonance.

It's like that for everyone. We're imprinted with unique preferences and experiences, which make up our own personal constellation of what success means. One friend of mine is obsessed with boats and barely sets foot on land during the summertime. I have problems with motion sickness and would rather die. Another colleague retreats to her country home every Friday afternoon, braving traffic to reach her oasis. But for me, having grown up with a family beach house that was the default destination for every vacation, the thought of going to the same location fifty times a year feels suffocating, not liberating.

We're all different. And that's why it's so powerful, finally, to reap the rewards of your effort and hard work—because the future you'll have created is unique to you, and exactly what you want.

Success—always—takes longer than we want. If we wait until we've finally "made it" to celebrate, we'll likely be waiting forever. After all, what is success? In ecology, there's a phenomenon known as *shifting baseline syndrome*. Over time and generations, we forget what the natural world around us used to be like. Dire and dramatically changed circumstances, like deforestation or the extinction of species, don't seem like such a big deal because, hey, hasn't it always been like this?

It's like that in our own lives, too. Early in our careers, we would have killed for some of the successes that we now experience and, at times, take for granted. You just closed a six-figure deal? Cool. You just published an article in that well-known publication? Nice. You just got invited to speak at such-and-such conference? Great.

Those are things that would have been worth a special dinner and calling all your friends years ago, but now they seem normal and basic. Your eyes are trained in front of you. Yeah, you were invited to speak, but you weren't the keynote. Yeah, you closed the deal, but you're not the biggest rainmaker in the firm. We forget what it was like to be us even a few years ago—and we forget how amazing our current success would have made us feel.

Becoming a recognized expert in your field, or achieving success of any kind, isn't a fast process. As we've seen throughout the book, it takes huge amounts of time and effort, and the emotional fortitude to withstand the inevitable setbacks. We can't keep it up if everything in our lives feels like an eternal slog. We have to find a way to tap into the magic. We have to show ourselves how far we've already come so we can see that the rest of the journey is possible.

OXOO

In the summer of 1996, between my junior and senior years of college, I landed an internship at the legendary advertising agency TBWA/Chiat/Day. The creator of Apple's iconic "1984" ad, it was renowned as one of the coolest in the nation. I was thrilled.

Every aspect of the experience was "on brand." Its downtown office, a showpiece frequently written up in business magazines at the time, had some of the usual high-end New York trappings, like a breathtaking view of the Statue of Liberty. But the agency innovated in ways that were unusual at the time. The office spanned two floors, and while you could take an elevator between them, you could also slide down the "Bat pole" that connected them. There was a room whose walls were covered with pillows, which you could hit if you were feeling frustrated—or, alternatively, you could cocoon there if that would help your creative process.

No one had a desk; it was one of the first examples of the open-office mania that would later sweep corporate America. Instead, you put your belongings in a locker each day and wandered around between open seating areas and conference rooms. But it wasn't a problem if people needed to reach out: you were issued a (primitive) cellular phone to use inside the office, back before almost anyone carried them regularly.

Working at the agency was a heady experience, and because of the hectic hours and intern-friendly food policy (if you worked past 7 p.m., you could order free delivery), I hardly left the building. That meant I never really got to know the downtown neighborhood where the office was located. In any case, the area seemed deserted after the workday ended—not a place that one really needed to explore.

Nearly two decades later, I decided to move to New York City. Certainly I'd visited since my one summer living there, but never for long. So when it was time to look for housing, I sent an email to my friends and colleagues in the city: Any tips? Any recommendations? One sent me, unexpectedly, to check out an apartment in the Financial District. Since 9/11, the neighborhood had reinvented itself. Corporate offices were still plentiful. But there had been an explosion of condo conversions and rental construction: it had become, to a surprising extent, a residential neighborhood.

The apartment building I visited seemed perfect. Constructed less than a decade before, it was modern and well-maintained, steps from the subway, and even had a gym and roof deck. I was in. It wasn't until I moved in several weeks later that I started to explore the neighborhood—and that's when I caught sight of something unexpected. It was a tall building by the waterfront, its glass exterior shimmering blue-green. It was the building I had worked in all those summers ago.

My new apartment building hadn't even been constructed back then, so I wouldn't have seen it. And in classic downtown New York style, the street names changed after a few blocks, so the address didn't ring a bell, either. But it turned out that my new residence was on the same street, not even two blocks away, as TBWA/Chiat/Day's former home.

It was a coincidence, of course. I ended up there on a random suggestion from a friend, and neighborhood demographics had changed following an unpredictable national tragedy. But New York is a big city—8.3 million people covering more than three hundred square miles—and I chose to see it as a sign. I chose to see it, every day when I'd leave my building and catch a glimpse of that skyscraper, as a personal reminder of how far I'd come in the intervening years. The failures, but also the successes: the books I'd written, the business I'd built, the life I'd created, the person I'd become. Even now, I walk past it nearly every day.

It's so easy to forget what we've accomplished. And when we do, we lose sight of the powerful fact that if we've done it before, we can do it again. With effort and enough of a horizon, almost anything is possible.

And that's true for any of us.

"I decided about five years ago that when I retire, I want to live in a cabin on a lake in a nice town and do part-time coaching," Samantha Fowlds told me. She's a Canadian executive and a member of my Recognized Expert course and community. "I realized that if I want that dream to come true in twenty years, then I have to start now so I will have a solid foundation. So three years ago, I earned my professional coaching designation, and now I take clients from time to time as I pursue my day job."

Unlike Samantha, most people never think that far ahead. They want something now, and get angry or frustrated when it doesn't immediately manifest. But the good things are ones you have to plan for—and work for.

In the short term, what gets you accolades—from family, from peers, from social media—is what's visible: the stable job, the beach vacation, the nice new car. It's easy to get swept along. No one ever gives you credit for doing what's slow and hard and invisible: sweating out that book chapter, doing that colleague a favor, writing that newsletter.

But we can't just optimize for the short term and assume that will translate into long-term success. We have to be willing to do hard, laborious, ungratifying things today—the kinds of things that make little sense in the short term—so we can enjoy exponential results in the future.

We have to be willing to be patient.

Not patient in a passive, "let things happen to you" way, but actively and vigorously patient: willing to deny yourself the easy path so you can do what's meaningful.

The results won't be visible tomorrow, when the progress you've made may be imperceptible. But they will be visible in five or ten or thirty years, when you've created the future you've always wanted. When you can look back on the skyscrapers where you used to work, and see how it's all come together.

Big goals often seem—and frankly are—impossible in the short term. But with small, methodical steps, almost anything is attainable. The *only* goal of this book has been to show you how to think, and act, for the long term, to make that possible.

Now it's up to you.

Remember:

We can train ourselves to be long-term thinkers using the following strategies:

- Get started in a very small way. Any goal can feel over-whelming if you look at it in its totality. But you'll create positive momentum if you start small and can see your success build.

- Understand what it really takes to accomplish your goals. Too many people get discouraged that they're not pro-gressing faster, simply because they never took the time to ask questions or discover how long it's taken others to succeed. Develop a clear picture first so you can pace yourself and set realistic goals.

- Setting constraints on the time you spend at work will, paradoxically, make you more efficient. You'll be forced to devise better systems and processes to manage your workflow.

- If you plan with a longer horizon than everyone else, and you're willing to endure the ups and downs along the way, you'll be able to accomplish far more than others—or even you—imagined.

Coda

Three Keys to Becoming a Long-Term Thinker

We'd all like to become more strategic thinkers—to rise above the clamor of the day-to-day, think deeply about our life and business goals, and attain the perspective and skills necessary to achieve them.

In this book, through research and the stories of real professionals, we've discussed a variety of strategies you can use to adopt a more strategic lens and embrace long-term thinking. You've learned about concepts like optimizing for interesting, thinking in waves, no asks for a year, infinite horizon networking, distance to empty, and more. But at the end of the day, what becoming a long-term thinker most requires is character.

It's the courage to carve your own path, without the reassurance of doing exactly what everyone else in the crowd is.

It's the willingness to look like a failure—sometimes for long periods—because it takes time for results to show.

And it's the strength to endure and persist, even when you aren't sure how it's going to turn out.

There are three habits of mind worth cultivating on your journey as a long-term thinker.

Independence. At its heart, long-term thinking is about staying true to yourself and your vision. In our society, there's so much pressure toward short-term people-pleasing: saying yes to one more commitment because you don't want to let someone down, or taking the "great job" that everyone else admires but that leaves you feeling dead inside. When you act for the long term, it can be quite a while before that pays off—and if you're looking outside yourself for validation, the wait can be devastating. To become fearless long-term thinkers, we need an internal compass that helps us say: "I'm willing to place my bet regardless of what others think, and I'm willing to do the work."

Curiosity. Some people are content to live their lives according to the road map that others have laid out for them, never questioning or pondering alternatives. But for many of us, a lifetime of coloring inside the lines can feel hollow, especially if our interests don't align with what society valorizes. We may not know the exact right path for ourselves (who does, at first?), but one quality that can lead us to it is curiosity. By noticing how we choose to spend our free time and understanding whom and what we find fascinating, we can pick up clues about what lights us up—and where, eventually, we can begin to make our contribution.

Resilience. Doing something new, something unique, is by definition experimental. You have no idea if it'll work or not—and oftentimes, it won't. Too many of us experience rejection or failure and immediately recoil, assuming that the editor who turned us down was the definitive arbiter of taste, or that the university that rejected us obviously knew what it was doing. But that's simply not true. Chance, luck, and individual preference play a massive role in how situations play out.

If one hundred people reject your work, that's a pretty clear message. But one or two or ten? You haven't even gotten started.

Becoming a long-term thinker requires a substratum of resilience, because it's rare that anything works out the first time or in the way you envisioned it. You need to have a plan B (or C, D, E, or F) in your back pocket, as well as the resilience to say: "Well, that didn't work, so let's try something else." Your number of at bats is the crucial variable in your success.

We all have the capability to hone our skills, develop new techniques, and become better long-term thinkers. It's my hope that this book has provided you with strategies you can use to start the journey—and even more important, to persevere so that you arrive at the exact destination you want.

Notes

Introduction

1. Martin Lindstrom, "Corporate America in Crisis! Would Thinking Like the Royals Solve a Big Problem?," LinkedIn, June 11, 2020, https://www.linkedin.com/pulse/corporate-america-crisis-would-thinking -like-royals-solve-lindstrom/.

2. https://dorieclark.com/rex.

Chapter 1

1. Robert Kabacoff, "Develop Strategic Thinkers throughout Your Organization," *Harvard Business Review*, February 7, 2014.

2. Rich Horwath, "The Strategic Thinking Manifesto," Strategic Thinking Institute, accessed March 9, 2021.

3. Michael Chui et al., "The Social Economy: Unlocking Value and Productivity through Social Technologies," McKinsey, July 1, 2012.

4. https://blog.hubspot.com/marketing/time-wasted-meetings-data.

5. Youngjoo Cha and Kim Weeden, "Overwork and the Slow Convergence in the Gender Gap in Wages," *American Sociological Review* 79, no. 3 (2014): 457-484.

6. John Pencavel, "The Productivity of Working Hours," *Economic Journal* 125, no. 589 (2015): 2052-2076.

7. Silvia Bellezza, Neeru Paharia, and Anat Keinan, "Research: Why Americans Are So Impressed by Busyness," *Harvard Business Review*, December 15, 2016.

8. Tim Ferriss, interview with Jerry Colonna, *The Tim Ferriss Show*, podcast audio, June 14, 2019.

9. Herbert A. Simon, "Designing Organizations for an Information-Rich World," in *Computers, Communications, and the Public Interest*, ed. Martin Greenberger (Baltimore: The Johns Hopkins Press, 1971).

Chapter 2

1. https://www.economist.com/news/1955/11/19/parkinsons-law.

2. https://sivers.org/hellyeah.

3. Frances Frei and Anne Morriss, *Uncommon Service* (Boston: Harvard Business Review Press, 2012).

Chapter 4

1. Larry Page and Sergey Brin, "An Owner's Manual for Google's Shareholders," 2004 founders' IPO letter, Google.

2. Nicholas Carlson, "The 'Dirty Little Secret' about Google's 20% Time, According to Marissa Mayer," *Business Insider*, January 13, 2015.

3. Jillian D'Onfro, "The Truth about Google's Famous '20% Time' Policy," *Business Insider*, April 17, 2015.

4. Owen Thomas, "Tesla's Elon Musk: 'I Ran Out of Cash,'" VentureBeat, May 27, 2010.

Chapter 5

1. Technically, the title is ambassador to the Court of St. James's.

2. The organization Thinkers50, which ranks the world's top business thinkers, has inducted Marshall into its Hall of Fame, making him the most highly lauded executive coach (https://thinkers50.com/biographies /marshall-goldsmith/).

Chapter 6

1. https://www.apa.org/science/about/psa/2009/10/sci-brief.

Chapter 7

1. Rick Hellman, "How to Make Friends? Study Reveals Time It Takes," KU News Service, University of Kansas, March 28, 2018.

2. https://www.jstor.org/stable/2776392?seq=1.

3. Carmen Nobel, "Professional Networking Makes People Feel Dirty," Working Knowledge, Harvard Business School, February 9, 2015.

4. Gladwell popularized the connector concept in his book *The Tipping Point*.

Chapter 8

1. https://www.insider.com/revealed-jk-rowlings-original-pitch-for-harry-potter-2017-10#:~:text=J.K.%20Rowling's%20pitch%20for%20'Harry, the%20now-famous%20letter%20here.

2. https://www.forbes.com/sites/alexknapp/2011/11/17/the-seduction-of-the-exponential-curve/#75ba0a072480.

3. https://www.amazon.com/dp/B00LD1RZGM/ref=dp-kindle-redirect?_encoding=UTF8&btkr=1.

4. Cathy Heller, interview with Derek Sivers, *Don't Keep Your Day Job*, podcast audio, December 23, 2019.

5. Eliot Van Buskirk, "Derek Sivers Sold CD Baby for $22 Million, Giving Most of It Away," *Wired*, October 24, 2008.

6. George Leonard, *The Way of Aikido: Life Lessons from an American Sensei* (Plume, 2000).

Chapter 9

1. https://www.pewresearch.org/fact-tank/2020/04/20/u-s-newsroom-employment-has-dropped-by-a-quarter-since-2008/.

Chapter 10

1. Keith Caulfield, "Lady Gaga Scores Sixth No. 1 Album on Billboard 200 Chart with 'Chromatica,'" Billboard, June 7, 2020.

2. Maria Konnikova, "The Struggles of a Psychologist Studying Self-Control," *The New Yorker*, October 9, 2014.

3. BJ Fogg, "Start Tiny," Tinyhabits.com, accessed March 9, 2021.

4. Jeff Bezos, "2017 Letter to Shareholders," About Amazon. Amazon, April 18, 2018, https://www.aboutamazon.com/news/company-news/2017 -letter-to-shareholders.

5. Steven Levy, "Jeff Bezos Owns the Web in More Ways Than You Think," *Wired*, November 13, 2011, https://static.longnow.org/media/djlongnow_media /press/pdf/020111113-Levy-JeffBezosOwnstheWebinMoreWaysThanYouThink .pdf.

Index

Further Resources

Throughout *The Long Game*, I've mentioned several complementary resources that might be helpful to you. They are:

Reinventing You. If you're contemplating a career change, you're in the midst of one, or you'd like to change how others perceive you, you might enjoy my first book, *Reinventing You*. It shows you how to take your "20% time" experiments and turn them into a more substantial part of how you spend your time and earn your revenue. Learn more at https://dorieclark.com/reinventingyou.

Stand Out. If there's an idea or a project or product you believe in, you want others to know about it. You want it to have a bigger impact. But in a noisy world, it's not always easy to figure out how. That's what *Stand Out* shows you how to do. If you've wondered how to raise your profile and get clients or potential employers or other opportunities to come to you, or how to spread the word about ideas you believe in, check out the book and learn more at https://dorieclark.com/stand-out.

Stand Out Networking. If you enjoyed chapter 7, "The Right People, the Right Rooms," you might also like this short ebook

I wrote about how to build authentic, long-term relationships—even if you're an introvert or dislike the concept of networking. Learn more at https://dorieclark.com/stand-out-networking.

Entrepreneurial You. This is a book for entrepreneurs and solopreneurs—current or aspiring—who want to learn how to develop new income streams. It's also useful for corporate employees who are interested in launching a side gig. If you enjoyed the discussion in *The Long Game* about how to develop strategic, low-risk career experiments with large potential upsides, *Entrepreneurial You* is worth checking out. I lay out strategies to help you learn how to start coaching or consulting on the side, and how to create passive income streams. Learn more at https://dorieclark.com/entrepreneurialyou.

Recognized Expert. If you're a professional—either self-employed or working inside a company—that wants to make a bigger impact and become a recognized expert in your field, this course is for you. Recognized Expert is both an intensive course (with more than fifty hours of high-quality content) and an active online community of more than six hundred smart and generous professionals. Becoming recognized for your expertise is all about playing the long game: it takes hard work, and it doesn't happen overnight. But as you've seen with the community members whose stories I share in this book, it's a powerful and worthwhile journey. Learn more and register at https://dorieclark.com/rex.

You can also download the free Recognized Expert self-assessment at https://dorieclark.com/toolkit. It will help you figure out where you are on your journey to becoming an expert and show you exactly how to accelerate your progress.

E-newsletter. If you'd like to stay in touch, please join the more than sixty-eight thousand readers I write to regularly by signing up for my e-newsletter at https://dorieclark.com/subscribe. *Forbes* has called my newsletter "an inspirational kick in the butt" that "inspires you to think deeper and challenge yourself." I try hard to make it entertaining and useful, so I hope you'll join!

Dorieclark.com. To access more than seven hundred free articles (which I've written for publications including *Harvard Business Review, Fast Company, Forbes, Entrepreneur,* the World Economic Forum blog, and more), as well as free self-assessments and resources, visit my website at https://dorieclark.com.

Acknowledgments

First and foremost, I could not have written this book without the friendship, encouragement, and inspiration provided by members of my Recognized Expert community. I'm especially grateful to the members who shared their insights and allowed me to tell their stories in this book.

A deep thank you to everyone I featured in *The Long Game*: your wisdom and your story will help countless others.

Thank you to my longtime agent, Carol Franco, and my incisive editors, Jeff Kehoe and Alicyn Zall, for making this book possible. I'd like to express my gratitude to Stephani Finks for her patience and hard work in the cover design process; Julie Devoll and Felicia Sinusas for promoting the book and creating an exceptional launch; and Victoria Desmond, Josh Olejarz, and other members of the *Harvard Business Review* team for their efforts in enabling *The Long Game* to come to fruition.

My talented assistant, Jon Hugo Ungar, provided invaluable help in enabling me to focus on the book while knowing that the rest of my business was in good hands.

As always, I'm grateful to my mother, Gail Clark, and to Ann Thomas for their love and support, and to close friends who always provide wise counsel, including Alisa Cohn, Jenny Blake, Shama Hyder, Petra Kolber, Joel Gagne, and so many others I hold in my heart, including the late Patty Adelsberger.

I would be remiss in not mentioning my amazing cats Phillip and Heath. Phil spent Covid Zoombombing enough hours to earn his Actors' Equity card and is currently seeking representation for stage, film, television, and endorsement opportunities.

Visit https://petfinder.com to find a beautiful homeless pet you can adopt.

About the Author

DORIE CLARK helps individuals and companies get their best ideas heard in a crowded, noisy world. She has been named one of the Top 50 management thinkers in the world by Thinkers50. She was honored as the #1 Communication Coach in the world by the Marshall Goldsmith Leading Global Coaches Awards, and one of the Top 10 Communication Professionals in the World by Global Gurus.

Clark teaches executive education at Duke University's Fuqua School of Business and at Columbia Business School. In addition, she speaks and consults for clients such as Google, the Bill & Melinda Gates Foundation, and the World Bank. A former presidential campaign spokesperson, Clark is the author of *Entrepreneurial You*, *Reinventing You*, and *Stand Out*, which was named the #1 Leadership Book of the Year by *Inc.* magazine.

Clark has been described by the *New York Times* as an "expert at self-reinvention and helping others make changes in their lives." She is a frequent contributor to *Harvard Business Review*, a producer of a multiple Grammy-winning jazz album, and a graduate of Harvard Divinity School.

You can download your free Long Game Strategy Self-Assessment at dorieclark.com/thelonggame.